THREE PLAYS

By the same author

Poems
Fishermen with Ploughs
Loaves and Fishes
The Year of the Whale
Winterfold
Selected Poems
Voyages

Short Stories
A Calendar of Love
A Time to Keep
Hawkfall
The Sun's Net
Andrina

Play
A Spell for Green Corn

Novels
Greenvoe
Magnus

Essays
An Orkney Tapestry
(Gollancz)
Letters from Hamnavoe
(Gordon Wright Publishing)
Under Brinkie's Brae
(Gordon Wright Publishing)

Non-Fiction
Portrait of Orkney
(with photographs by Werner Forman)

For Children
The Two Fiddlers
Pictures in the Cave
Six Lives of Fankle the Cat

THREE PLAYS

by George Mackay Brown

THE LOOM OF LIGHT, THE WELL *and* THE VOYAGE OF SAINT BRANDON

CHATTO & WINDUS · THE HOGARTH PRESS

LONDON

Published in 1984 by
Chatto & Windus The Hogarth Press
40 William IV Street
London WC2N 4DF

British Library
Cataloguing in Publication Data
Brown, George Mackay
  Three plays.
  I. Title
  822'.914   PR6052.R/

ISBN 0–7011–2742–2

The publisher acknowledges subsidy
from the Scottish Arts Council towards
the publication of this volume

Phototypeset by
Wyvern Typesetting Limited, Bristol
Printed in Great Britain by
The Camelot Press Ltd
Southampton

To STEWART CONN

Contents

Preface

The Loom of Light was staged in 1972 in the new Arts Theatre, Kirkwall, Orkney, at a time when funds were being raised for the preservation of St Magnus Cathedral in Kirkwall. After eight centuries 'the wonder and glory of the north' was showing signs of strain and wear. The director was David Birch and a few of the characters were played by professional actors, but most were Orcadians.

In an anthology compiled by Herbert Read for servicemen in the Second World War, called *The Knapsack*, I discovered with delight the medieval account of the voyage of St Brandon [Brendan], sixth-century abbot of Clonfert, in quest of 'the island of the blessed'. It seemed to me that it would make a good play for voices. I worked at it, on and off, for a few years. It is being produced by Stewart Conn on Radio 4 at Easter 1984: than which there could be no better time for a play like *Brandon*. That fine actor Cyril Cusack plays Brandon, and Thomas Wilson has woven beautiful music into it.

The Well was specially written for the St Magnus Festival of midsummer 1981, with Ernie Donaldson directing a cast of Orkney players. Round a well above a shore I tried to gather as much Orkney legend and history as I thought entertaining, mysterious, and instructive. Peter Maxwell Davies wrote incidental music; around one of the later scenes he wove fuller music, in a piece called *Into the Labyrinth*, that was first performed at the St Magnus Festival of 1983.

Since its first performance, I have completely re-written the last scene.

Readers might be interested to learn, briefly, how *The Loom of Light* grew and developed. It began with the last scene only, which was a kind of coda to the prose account of St Magnus' rule and martyrdom that appeared in *An Orkney Tapestry* (Gollancz, 1969).

Then it seemed logical to cast the whole 'biography' in dramatic form: hence *The Loom of Light*.

Some writers are never content to leave well alone. On to the stark framework of the play I rigged the novel *Magnus* (The Hogarth Press,

1973); making as full use as possible of the more varied techniques at the novelist's disposal. And of course the work was enormously enriched when Peter Maxwell Davies made use of the text and setting and dialogue for his chamber opera *The Martyrdom of Saint Magnus*, which has been performed in churches and minsters all over Europe. Appropriately, the opera had its first performance at the first St Magnus Festival, and within the walls of St Magnus Cathedral itself, with the composer conducting.

George Mackay Brown
November 1983

THE LOOM OF LIGHT

Scene I SEEDTIME

CHORUS
The year 1075 since Bethlehem and Herod.

There is a king in Norway, who is king also of Orkney, Shetland, Caithness, the Hebrides, Man, all the broken coastlines of the west.

In Orkney the king keeps two earls, black earl and red earl.

In winter, once the harvest is in, the earls move ivory chessmen beside a fire in the Hall.

The croft women turn perpetual wheels of wool and stone and malt.

The monks in a green holm sing every day the sevenfold office. They wear the long bright coats of chastity, poverty, obedience.

It is spring – the red earl will sanctify desire with ceremony. And in spring fishermen and peasants go out to break the new furrows, salt and clay.

The springtime of the year 1075. The flank of Revay Hill in Birsay. Across a narrow sleeve of water, on a steep tidal island, is the palace of the earl of Orkney and also the small cathedral church of the bishop of Orkney. There are some women down at the shore waiting for the tide to ebb. Two peasants, Mans and his wife Hild, are breaking the virgin earth of the hillside with mattocks.

HILD Fancy asking us to work on a day like this. It's a shame. It really is, Mans.

MANS Peasants must work till they drop dead. That's what peasants are for.

HILD And the hill full of stones, too. How will we ever be able to sow seed in this . . .

MANS 'Mans,' he says to me, 'I want you to plough out a new bit of hill tomorrow morning. It'll be tough work,' says he, 'but you're the strongest man in Birsay' . . . I hate that factor.

HILD Today of all days. I want so much to see the wedding.

MANS 'I can't do that,' I said to him. 'O and why not?' says he.

3

'Because,' I said, 'my ox is lame' . . . 'O,' says he, 'is that so? Well (says he) what's wrong with Hild? she's a strong young woman. Yoke her.'

CHORUS

Go back, water. The sea is brimming and large.
Go back now from crags and seapinks.
We want to cross over
To see a marvellous thing in the kirk today,
The marriage of the lord Erlend
To the lady Thora of Paplay.
Go back, bitterness and coldness, soon
From the small wet stones.

HILD *crying out* Oh!

MANS What's wrong now?

HILD I struck another stone, Mans. The pain went up my arm like a flame.

MANS I hate that man. 'What's wrong with Hild? Yoke her . . .' But of course he's only doing what he's told to do. There's worse than him.

A bell sounds once, sweetly, on the island.

HILD Listen, Mans. That's the start of the wedding.

MANS That's got nothing to do with us. Get on with your work. Stop talking. The factor's bad enough. But there's worse than him . . .

He picks up a stone.

Look at this stone. How do they expect barley from a wilderness like this?

He throws the stone away.

HILD My back's nearly broken.

A young tinker man and his woman appear.

MANS I'll tell you who's worse than the factor. The bishop who owns half the fields. And the two earls who own the other half. They're worse. To them we're just beasts. There's a worse one than them still, and that's the king of Norway.

4

HILD *warningly* Sh – h – h, Mans. *She looks around.* Somebody might hear you. We're peasants. God called us to be poor people. It's not for us to complain. The bishop is a good kind man, I don't care what you say.

MANS Save your breath for the digging.

CHORUS
Go back, water. Begin to shrink.
Quickly go back from the small wet stones.
The bell is ringing.
The girls have put a long white gown on the bride.
Go back, drowner of men
From the wrack and the rockpools.

MANS *throwing away his mattock.* Dinner time, woman. What's in the basket?

Hild puts down her mattock, straightens herself, goes over to a rock and brings a jar of ale and a bannock and cheese. Mans takes them from her: he breaks the bannock and gives the smaller bit to Hild. Mans eats sitting with his back to the rock. Hild eats standing in the broken earth. The timkers watch them wordlessly, their hands half out, saying nothing.

A bell rings from the steeple.

HILD *before eating, makes a cross over her food* Bless us, Lord, and these thy gifts to us from thy bounty.

MANS 'What's wrong with your wife?' says he – 'Yoke her . . .' The swine . . . Who's getting married today, anyway?

HILD O Mans, you know quite well. It's the lady Thora and the lord Erlend, Earl Thorfinn's son.

MANS Are they? You know who'll have to pay for that lot – you and me. You and me and the poor folk of Orkney. It's us that'll pay for that wedding. We'll keep the silk on their backs and the wine in their cups. Parasites.

He spits.

HILD It's a shame, it really is. Look at the women down at the shore. They're waiting to cross over once it ebbs. A lovely wedding. And here we are breaking out this hill. This day of all days. It's a shame.

5

MANS Parasites. *He points to the island.* Look at the palace they live in, compared to our hovels. They have a fine easy life, with their hawks and their harps and their fancy-women. They get bored with that sometimes. Then the two earls decide to have a little war. They knock hell out of each other for a winter or two. Or rather, poor Mans the peasant and poor Anders the fisherman, they knock hell out of each other. The earls sit back and watch from their high windows. Pass the bottle.

HILD *as the church bells ring out joyously.*
There she goes now, the bride! Lady Thora. Out of the palace and into the kirk. And her three girls with her. She's lovely as a swan!

Hild holds out a crust to the tinkers. The woman tinker, Mary, comes across swift as a shadow and takes it.

MANS Yes, in wartime it's the poor who get the sword in their guts, not them. It's the poor who have to pay for their wars with taxes ... *He suddenly notices the tinkers.* Get away from here. Go on now. There's nothing here for you.

HILD There is a drop left in the jar.

MANS Not for tinks. Clear off. We're busy. *He drinks the rest of the jar of ale, rises, wipes his mouth.* Clear to hell.

The tinkers go off down towards the shore, where the burn is supple with trout, where, once it ebbs, there is the chance of cake and wine left over from the wedding.

Jock and Mary pay no attention to the ceremony. They wander about the shore looking for sticks to make a fire; between now and sundown there is a possibility of stewed rabbit.

CHORUS
Go back, water.
Ebb from wrack and shells and rockpools.
We have brought small gifts
To lay at the door of the bride.
Go back, bearer of whales and ships.
Leave only a scatter of rockpools.
We will cross over now
With rapt wet feet to the Temple of Love.

6

Mans and Hild strike the hillside, one after the other, painfully and ritually.

The nuptial Mass begins in Christ Church.

The women of Birsay begin to cross over to the island.

MANS All parasites.

While Mans is ranting and opening the hill slowly, Hild drops her mattock and goes down to join the other women who are going now from stone to stone among the rockpools with raised skirts.

MANS Next winter there'll be another lordly mouth in the island. Who'll feed it? I'll tell you. Mans and Hild, they'll feed the brat. The poor folk of Orkney, they'll have to feed it all its life by the sweat of their brows. Yes, with the plough . . . and with the seed basket . . . and with the scarecrow . . . and with a scythe . . . and with flails . . . and with quernstones . . . and with kilns and fires . . . We'll keep the bite in your mouth, little earl, never fear. Till it's too dark to work any more and our bones are broken.

The sun is going down. Chant of the choristers. Tall in the last of the light, Mans strikes and strikes, opening the virgin hill with his rage and brute strength. There is a flicker among the rocks – the tinkers have lit a fire.

The women stretch their necks like swans in the door of the church.

The bishop has put the ring on the bride's finger.

MANS *in the twilight.* Yes, till we're all dead and we don't need to slave any more . . . Hild. Where are you, woman? I told you not to go to the church. I need my supper. *He shouts over to the island* Come home now, at once!

BISHOP *at the church door, blessing the bridegroom and bride.* Benedicat vos Omnipotens Deus, Pater et Filius et Spiritus Sanctus.

MANS *throwing down his mattock under the first star* I'll thrash her within an inch of her life . . . The parasites – I hope they're all sick as dogs in the morning. *He goes home.*

7

It is completely dark in Birsay now. Presently a light goes on in the palace, then a cluster of lights in the great chamber, there is a mingling of harps and pipes and a hundred festive voices.

[BRIDAL SONG]
 What guests stand at the door of the Hall?
 The king's man, in cloth of gold,
 A skipper coated in blue and gray,
 A farmer, in green and saffron,
 All their women, hued like rainbows.
 (Better those festal coats
 Than what the loom of war gives out,
 The shrouds patched with red.)
 All go in, among the harps and candles.
 A fishwife shawled in gray
 Leaves a basket of haddock at the wall.
 The hodden croft-wife
 Has left a jug of ale at the door.
 The poor of Orkney
 Have no part in the circling bridal dance.
 The ragged tinkers leave nothing, as yet.
 Moths eat the candles, the axe has a flake of rust.
 The harp's tongue is pure and sweet.

The light in the nuptial chamber is lost in the light of a new day and another springtime.

The tinkers come up from the shore.

MARY Listen to that lark, Jock. He's lost in the sun now. No, he's not. I see him there, in the heart of the sun, quivering, look, like the point of a needle.

JOCK You're too fond of bright things, Mary. Stars. Honeycombs. Rockpools. Come on. We must be in Orphir when the alehouse opens.

Mans and Hild come in, Mans with a seed-basket slung over his shoulder.

MANS *to the tinkers* Get away, vagabonds. Don't stand in that furrow. I

8

have to grow bread there this summer. Off with you.

HILD Sh – h – h, Mans. They'll put the evil eye on us.

The tinkers drift out on the spring wind.

MANS I'm not frightened of the likes of them . . . We'll have to work hard today, Hild. There's that new mouth to feed in the palace over there.

HILD He was christened this morning. The Bishop called him MAGNUS.

Mans throws a first fist-ful of seed into the broken earth.

[BRIDAL SONG: conclusion]
Listen: somewhere a loom is set
Beyond moth and rust.
Fall, tissue of peace, from the loom,
A single fold of light,
That the just man
May walk at last in a white coat among this people.

Scene 2 A BOY AND A SEAL

Ten years pass: ten turnings of snow and seed to the fecund sun.

The western horizon belongs to the king of Norway alone; no other sail breaks the huge circle.

In Orkney, black earl and red earl match hawks, one against the other.

The ladies draw long coloured threads through their stretched linen. Croft women sew patches.

The monks in a green holm sing every day the seven-fold office. They wear the long bright coats. To innocence they impart, page by page, holy instruction.

The fisherman brings to his door one cod out of seven.

The cathedral on Birsay island. The clergy have here a school for the sons of the northern gentry. The bishop, alone, with his breviary. Brother Colomb, an elderly cleric and dominie, comes in.

BROTHER COLOMB The new pupils, my lord. They're crossing over from the Birsay shore now. Brother Fergus is meeting them.

BISHOP The tide is out?

BROTHER COLOMB Yes, Father.

BISHOP Brother Colomb, I have a list of their names here. It makes interesting reading. Listen. *He reads* Magnus Erlendson, Havard Gunison, Sigurd Kolison, Hakon Paulson, Hold Ragnarson, Sighvat Sokk, Finn Thorkelson.

BROTHER COLOMB *nodding* Magnus Erlendson, Hakon Paulson.

BISHOP The two future earls of Orkney – the red earl and the black earl.

A brief silence.

BROTHER COLOMB The two lips of the wound.

BISHOP That wound has been open for a long time. It'll take some healing. That wound has bled Orkney to death almost.

BROTHER COLOMB Surely the business of politics is the health and healing of a people, not wounds.

BISHOP No. The King of Norway needs an open wound in the west. A whole sound Orkney – that would make an independent music. Very well, the king must wound the harp, and keep wounding it, again and again. Instead of one earl in the islands, Norway always insists on two. Two earls to rule over a few islands – what nonsense! The coat-of-state riven – the earls going in half a coat each, rich shameful beggars . . . There is not room here for two earls. They start off with the best of intentions, in their double yoke. 'O yes, we will rule well, justly, fairly'. It always happens, of course, that one gains the upper hand. There is a strong earl and a weak earl. The weak one carries his complaints east to Norway. From the king he gets money, ships, men. He sits at the king's fire all winter. In spring he sails west again, the king's particular man. The earldom shrieks like a riven harp from end to end. So Orkney, poor Orkney, bleeds from generation to generation, to keep this 'pax borealis' in existence . . . I'm sorry. Is there anything else?

BROTHER COLOMB The seal on the rock, Father. He's very sick. I think he'll die before tonight.

BISHOP There *could* be something in what you are thinking, Colomb. The two future earls of Orkney are coming here today. In their innocence they are coming to Birsay. They are bringing that old wound to the brothers for a year or two.

We will see what a little ghostly surgery can do.

Six boys stand in the door.

BROTHER COLOMB The new pupils, my lord.

BISHOP Leave me alone with them for a minute.

BROTHER COLOMB I will . . . *To one of the boys* Stop snivelling. You had to leave your mother sometime. *To the others* Over here. Don't keep his lordship waiting. *He goes out*

The new pupils stand scrubbed, curious, and uncertain, before the bishop.

BISHOP Did you get your feet wet in the seaweed?

BOYS *together* No, Father.

SIGHVAT SOKK I did. My feet are soaked through.

BISHOP I am the bishop here in Birsay. *The boys bow respectfully*. I want
first to know your names – your fathers' names – the places you
come from . . . Then it will be dinner-time. Brother Colomb will be
giving you a timetable, I expect. Colomb, that means dove, but if you
don't attend to your lessons you'll find he's anything but a dove. *He
smiles* He's a good man, all the same. He wants you to learn well the
things of God and man. *He puts a hand on Sighvat's shoulder* Salt water is
wholesome water. It won't hurt you. You can dry your feet at the
fire.

You're to be here, in Birsay, for three years. You'll learn many
mysteries – writing, music, Latin, algebra, verse-making. There'll
be plenty of time too for such things as fishing, sailing, swimming,
cliff-climbing. Most important of all, you must learn how to bear
yourselves courteously among all men everywhere, in a way pleasing
to God.

Now, your names. First *pointing to a boy* you.

FINN THORKELSON Finn. I come from Hoy. My father is
Thorkel. He lives in The Bu there. My mother and my three sisters,
they live there too. There's fifteen women servants.

BISHOP Finn, this is a place of men entirely. You'll miss the little
sisters. Here no one speaks very much.

FINN THORKELSON It will make a good change, Father.

BISHOP *to the second boy* And you?

HAKON PAULSON My lord, you know me. I've been in this island a
hundred times.

BISHOP Your name, please.

HAKON PAULSON Hakon. My father is Paul, earl of Orkney. His
father was Thorfinn earl of Orkney. His father before him was
Sigurd, earl of Orkney. The father of Earl Sigurd –

BISHOP Thank you, Hakon Paulson. That will be enough. All the
boys are equal here. *To the next boy* Your name?

HOLD RAGNARSON Hold.

BISHOP And your father's name?

HOLD RAGNARSON Ragnar. From Ness in the Hebrides. He died
last winter.

BISHOP Do you like being here, Hold Ragnarson?

HOLD RAGNARSON No.

BISHOP You'll come to like it, I'm sure. *To the next boy* And you?

HAVARD GUNISON Havard Gunison. Guni, she's my mother. My father's a useless kind of man. He sits at the fire all winter – he plays chess and he strums a harp. He hasn't had a sword in his hand for twelve years.

BISHOP We could do with more of his kind in Orkney. *To the fifth boy.* You, boy, lift your head.

But this boy – he is the one Brother Colomb told to stop snivelling – will not look; he is too overcome with home-sickness; he sees vividly the loch and the mill and the wild horses on the moor.

BISHOP I want your name.

No answer.

HOLD RAGNARSON I think he's called Sigurd Kolison, my lord.

BISHOP You with the wet feet, what about you?

SIGHVAT SOKK Sighvat. I come from Westray. My father has three ships there. We only see him in winter. He's a viking.

BISHOP Let me see. That's only six of you. There should be another boy.

FINN THORKELSON Another boy crossed over with us. We left him among the rocks. He wouldn't come in.

The Bishop goes to the window, leans out, and calls.

BISHOP Boy! . . . You there. You must come in at once to be enrolled.

On the sea-banks a boy whistles. He utters some words. The words scatter in the vastness

BISHOP *turning back into the church* He's calling to the seals. Do any of you know that boy?

HAKON PAULSON I know him. He's my cousin Magnus Erlendson. He comes from Paplay in Holm.

BISHOP *at the window, calling* Boy, come here, your class is about to begin.

13

MAGNUS ERLENDSON *outside* It's too dark in there. I can't come
inside yet. There's a seal hurt, down at the rock. I'm trying to reach
him. I might be able to help him.

BISHOP But won't you tell me your name?

A face appears at the door in the sunlight. The wind sifts bright hair.

MAGNUS ERLENDSON O yes, Father. I'm Magnus. I come from
Paplay in Holm. My father is earl of Orkney.

HAKON PAULSON *shouting* Earl of Orkney – you liar! *My* father is
earl of Orkney. Your father is only the brother of my father.

BISHOP *to Hakon Paulson, sharply* Be quiet! Here no one shouts like
that. *He turns to the face at the door.* Won't you come in, Magnus
Erlendson, and meet the other boys?

MAGNUS ERLENDSON Not till the seal is well. Somebody has cut
him with an axe. His coat's all blood.

*The face withdraws from the door. There is the noise of loose stones as feet move off down
the beach.*

HAKON PAULSON Father, I'll go out and I'll drag Magnus
Erlendson in. I'm his cousin. I know him. He'll do what I say.

BISHOP You will stay where you are.

Brother Colomb stands at the inner door.

BISHOP Brother Colomb is ready for you.

BROTHER COLOMB *pointing along the corridor* That way. The refectory's at the end of the passage. There's trout for dinner. In the
afternoon I will try to teach you some Latin.

*The boys file out past Brother Colomb. Sigurd Kolison takes away his grief-dappled
face.*

BROTHER COLOMB *to the bishop.* Those wanderers were here again.
There's something wrong with the woman's eyes. I put a tincture in
them . . . What's that?

Colomb has heard a new noise among the island noises: Magnus speaking to the seal.

BISHOP We have a truant, Colomb. Not a wild one – a gentle one,

Magnus Erlendson. See that Magnus Erlendson doesn't steal your
name from you. Listen.

The sound of whistling far off, under the cliff, then laughter, then a seal's muted pain.
They all come trembling across the great harp of the sea.

BISHOP I forgot to say, Colomb – the king of Norway has a more
drastic way of holding his empire together. He carries war into
Ireland and England. All the vassal earls are compelled to follow
him. That way they learn glory and obedience at the same time.

MAGNUS ERLENDSON *singing at the island shore*
Come from the rock now, cold one.
See, I have a fish for you in my hand.
My name is Magnus.
I have told the hunters to leave this shore.
There is a wound in your head.
If you do not come to me soon you will die.
Your blood will grow cold as shells.
Rats and crabs will cover your beautiful coat.

BISHOP How will it be with that one out there, I wonder, when the
swords and axes are sharpened?

Scene 3   SONG OF BATTLE

CHORUS

Thirteen years pass. Boys have grown into men. They ride to the
harbour with hawks in their fists.

The king of Norway gathers his empire about him like a rich coat
that is always coming apart; stitches work loose here and there.
From Iceland, Faroe, Shetland, Orkney, Caithness, the Hebrides,
Ireland, Man, the ships gather.

In Orkney, Hakon Paulson and Magnus Erlendson put aside
chessmen and hawks. They sail with the king into the Irish Sea, they
also. Norway will cut a new and weightier coat from the unrolling
web of history.

In the islands, women wait at the shore.

The monks in a green holm sing every day the seven-fold office.
They wear the long bright coats. Their war is with principalities and
powers, the lords of darkness.

It is summer. A peasant here and there has left the slow surge of
the hills; he's an oarsman now; a quick sea-dazzle is in his eyes.

*The Menai Strait, between Anglesey and Wales. A Norse ship in cold hard
light. A Welsh ship appearing out of the fog.*

*The king of Norway sits in the stern of his ship with Norwegian, Danish,
Hebridean, Icelandic, Orkney shields all about him. His face is armoured so
that he seems to be wearing a silver mask.*

*Magnus Erlendson is seated in the bow. He is reading out of a psalter
aloud. 'Why take ye thought for raiment? Consider the lilies of the field, how
they grow. They toil not neither do they spin. And yet I say unto you that
even Solomon in all his glory was not arrayed like one of these . . .*

*Here and there in the Norse ship we can pick out known faces: Sigurd
Kolison, Hakon Paulson, Hold Ragnarson, Sighvat Sokk, Finn Thorkelson. The ship turns into the sun – the faces redden and blanch – the silver
mask flashes.*

*Heralds – men with inviolate sacred mouths – stand in the prow of each
ship.*

A horn is blown on the Norse ship.

NORSE HERALD Men in the Celtic ship.

WELSH HERALD We are listening, strangers.

NORSE HERALD This is a narrow channel. There is not enough room, I think, for two ships to pass.

WELSH HERALD That is true. It is our channel, Menai. Go back.

NORSE HERALD What is the name of the land behind you?

WELSH HERALD Anglesey. An island of corn and cattle.

Women stand at the shore of Anglesey watching the ships.

NORSE HERALD We will land there. We need bread and women.

WELSH HERALD We Welsh know how to trade with merchants like you. Shoot!

In the Welsh ship bows are raised. Arrows point at the Norse ship. A Norseman falls.

MANS THE BIRSAY PEASANT *to his fellow oarsmen* I wish to God I was home on Revay Hill. *Mans tries to hide under the thwart.*

NORSE HERALD Welshmen, listen. Take the filth out of your ears.

WELSH HERALD Our ears are like shells.

NORSE HERALD Your arrows have struck one of our men: Arni the weaver, from Yell in Shetland, is dead.

WELSH HERALD It will be a threadbare winter in the Shetlands – but not so cold as for Arni.

NORSE HERALD Archers, argue with them. My tongue is tired.

A horn. In the Norse ship the warriors raise bows. Arrows point at the Welsh ship. Two Welshmen fall.

MAGNUS ERLENDSON *reading out of his psalter* 'Thou preparest a table before me in the presence of my enemies. Thou anointest my head with oil. My cup runneth over . . .'

The Norse ship advances.

WELSH HERALD Not too near, hawk heads, for the spears.

The Welsh warriors point spears at the Norse ship. Two Norsemen fall.

NORSE HERALD You have killed Finn and Thord, farmers in Iceland.

WELSH HERALD They will grow seaweed this summer. They will rear crabs.

NORSE HERALD Who is the black ugly man sitting in the highest thwart?

WELSH HERALD Hugh, earl of Shrewsbury, is in our ship.

NORSE HERALD We have come all this way to talk with a man called Hugh the Proud.
　　Speak, spears.

A horn. Spears are raised on the Norse ship. They glint in the sun. They point at the Welsh ship. Three Welshmen fall.

WELSH HERALD Well hunted, hawks. You have a certain luck in matters of death.

NORSE HERALD The falconry has only begun.

WELSH HERALD Who is the fat man with the silver mask? He is half hidden in shields.

NORSE HERALD The king of Norway is in these parts.

WELSH HERALD Some kings are a long time getting home. The queen watches. The sea is empty.

NORSE HERALD The Welshman has a bitter tongue. Speak with him nearer. Turn the ship, helmsman.

The ships close. They are tangled in sun and mist.

WELSH HERALD Now it is axes.

NORSE HERALD Now it is swords and axes and fire.

MAGNUS ERLENDSON 'The king's daughter is all glorious within. Her clothing is of wrought gold. She shall be brought in to the king in raiment of needlework . . .'.

The Celtic warriors stand broadside, a rank of ghosts. The Norse warriors stand in a bright wedge aimed at the centre of the Welsh ship.

WELSH HERALD What men besides the king have come down from the north for this battle? We have a bard on our ship. He wishes to list their names in our song of victory.

NORSE HERALD Vidkunn. Sigurd. Serk. Dag. Arn. Eyvind. Ogmund. Finn and Thord. Koli. Hakon the son of Paul who is earl in Orkney, Magnus the son of Erlend who is earl in Orkney.

MAGNUS ERLENDSON *reading* 'Who is this that cometh from Edom, with dyed garments from Bosra, this beautiful one in his robe, walking in the greatness of his strength?'

WELSH HERALD Who is the young man who is fighting this battle with a psalter?

NORSE HERALD Magnus of Orkney is here. I told you.

HAKON PAULSON *shouting* There is a coward in every battle!

WELSH HERALD A coward would be hiding under the thwart. A coward doesn't sit in the teeth of the swords.

NORSE HERALD There is too much talking in this battle.

WELSH HERALD It will come to silence soon enough.

The Norsemen with raised axes advance with slow ritualistic paces. They breach the Welsh line. The fog glints, the sunlight is tarnished. One after another the Welshmen fall, or kneel. Hugh, earl of Shrewsbury, comes before the king of Norway; he kneels; he offers his sword.

WELSH HERALD The Menai Strait is yours, Norway.

NORSE HERALD We will cast anchor. We will provision our ships. We will make a passage.

WELSH HERALD Thy queen will see thee once more, Norway. Some day you will not go back to her.

The horn sounds thrice. The battle is over. The Norsemen raise their loot into the light – silver, tapestries, harps, rings.

MANS Look what I've got for Hild – a brooch!

AN OARSMAN There's blood on your knee, mate.

MANS *screeching* I'm wounded! I'm crippled for life! I wish I was home! I have a croft to work. They tried to kill me.

Mans sits on the bench and clasps his knee.

MAGNUS ERLENDSON 'The coat that Israel gave to his beloved son, Joseph, a beautiful garment of many colours, it was taken from him. Steeped in the blood of beasts it became one colour . . .'

HAKON PAULSON *to Magnus* Coward. Fool. Hypocrite.

Magnus Erlendson puts down his psalter. He tears the sleeve from his fine white linen shirt.

NORSE HERALD A proclamation from the hand of the King of Norway to the princes and chiefs of the west. *A horn.* Let the chroniclers and sagamen record that in the year of Our Lord 1098 in the month of June a great and famous victory was gained by Norway at sea over the princes and lords of Wales. Let it be brightly written on the scrolls.

Magnus Erlendson kneels in front of Mans the peasant oarsman. He binds his wound with the torn piece of shirt.

MAGNUS ERLENDSON *binding Mans' wound* Another wound. You'll have a silver scar and a limp. But you'll reap a few harvests yet.

NORSE HERALD Further, let this be proclaimed – all the islands in the west of Britain are under the hand of Norway, from Faroe to Scilly. Of all those islands Orkney is the chiefest earldom. We confirm that our servant Paul is earl in Orkney and that his brother our servant Erlend is earl in Orkney also. May they govern long in our peace and favour. And we declare that after Paul and Erlend there shall rule in Orkney Hakon, son of Paul, and Magnus the psalm-singer, son of Erlend and Thora: these two, right leal and sweet and trusty servants, woven into the one great music of the North . . .

The Welsh ship burns, a gout of red, through the fog.

Magnus Erlendson returns to his coat and psalter.

Ghostly shawled figures appear through the swirls – the women of Anglesey moving among their dead.

WOMEN OF ANGLESEY
Our curse upon the bright-haired strangers.
May the agony they have brought to Wales return upon their heads.
Let their furrows soak with blood.

Wives, mothers, sweethearts of Orkney
Remember this day ·
When your cut cornstalks ooze blood,
When foreign horsemen sleep in your barns.

Scene 4 THE FIELDS IN SUMMER

CHORUS
Seventeen years pass, a time steeped in the vats of war. Homeward
the bitter flagons are borne.

The king of Norway consults with an ambassador, a merchant,
seven spies.

Earl Paul and Earl Erlend are dead. The two new earls, Hakon
and Magnus, sit at opposite ends of Orkney, and this is the kind of
chessmen they manipulate – fire, axe, noose, arrow, winged helmet.
The hawk is out of the heraldry now, it is hung free, a hunter, a
hoverer with dripping hooks.

Women sew shrouds. The spade of the gravedigger glitters.

The monks in a green holm sing every day the seven-fold office.
Through the reddening warp they weave incessant sounds of peace.
They wear the long bright coats.

The peasants are no longer required. After the death of the seed
the corn is killed a second time. Foreign horsemen ride through the
smashed furrows.

*The cultivated side of Revay Hill in Birsay. In Mans' and Hild's field a
scarecrow stands among the first green corn – a cross with a rigging of rags.*

*A man with a bell and a parchment enters. He stands among the fields. He strikes his bell
once. He reads:*

THE MAN WITH THE BELL 'TAKE NOTICE, peasants of Orkney,
in particular those within the parish of Birsay – a PROCLAMATION
signed by the one true earl of Orkney MAGNUS ERLENDSON: In
consequence of the war levied within our bounds by Hakon Paulson
and those traitorously adhering to him, and having regard to the
high cost of containing and putting down the rebellion, you are
herewith advised that your earldom rents will be increased to a sack
of barley meal and a stone of butter as from the summer solstice last.
GOD save THE KING and THE EARL'.

The bellman goes out. Hild comes in followed by Mans. They both search in the heather.

HILD You go back home, Mans. Bar the door. There's horsemen in the parish. I heard them this morning. I'll look for the hen myself.

MANS I'm not frightened of them.

HILD Go home now. Anders was taken for a soldier last week.

MANS I could do with a boiled egg all the same. I was never so hungry.

HILD *low sweet cajolery* Kittag kittag. The pretty good dear. Come to Hild, then. Chooky chook. There's a sweetheart.

Three mercenaries with black patches on their sleeves come in.

SOLDIER You there. Did you see a troop of red horsemen near here this morning?

MANS What horsemen?

SOLDIER Magnus Erlendson's horsemen.

MANS *sullenly* No.

HILD There were horsemen on the road above. Red patches on their coats. I heard hooves a while back.

SOLDIER This way. We must get to the crossroads before them.

The mercenaries go trampling over Mans' field.

MANS That's my field! Don't you know a cornfield? You're worse than the wild pigs.

HILD Be quiet, Mans.

MANS *following the mercenaries but not too close* You're tramping on the bread of the people!

The soldiers ride off regardless.

MANS *raging* Them and their wars! Hakon and Magnus, curse the pair of them! And their bloody foreign soldiers too – Norskys, Scots.

HILD Have patience, Mans. They'll come to their senses soon. If the war goes on much longer, the lairds will be as poor as we are.

MANS *plucking a stalk of grass and nibbling at it* Prem and me, we were speaking about it. I was up at Prem's last night. There was Prem sitting at his loom. I'll tell you what I said to Prem. 'Prem,' I said, 'we're one folk, us islanders, we belong to one another. Priest, ploughman, laird, tinker, fisherman, earl – we're all woven together into a kind of coat. A fine thick warm coat, like what you might go to kirk or market in. Now the coat's in pieces,' I said. 'Orkney is naked. Everybody trying to cover himself with his own bit of rag.'

Enter from the other side five helmeted mercenaries with axes and red patches sewn on their coats.

SOLDIER *to Mans, quietly* What are you shouting about?

MANS *crestfallen* Nothing.

HILD Nothing at all, sir. He put too much ale in his porridge this morning.

SOLDIER Drunkard, did you see a company of men on this hill? Men with black patches on their sleeves.

MANS I saw nothing.

HILD Soldiers passed down that way a little while ago. They had black patches. They barricaded themselves in the mill.

SOLDIER To the mill – we've got them!

The mercenaries begin to move off. One of them turns.

SOLDIER Wait a minute. What's that you've got in your apron, woman?

MANS Nothing.

SOLDIER I wasn't speaking to you, tosspot.

HILD A couple of eggs, sir. My old black hen, she comes and she lays eggs in the heather here.

SOLDIER The lieutenant here is hungry. He's had no breakfast.

HILD I'm going to clip her wings, that's what I'm going to do.

SOLDIER *holding out his palm* What about the lieutenant's breakfast, eh?

MANS *muttering* The bishop will hear about this.

The soldier takes a dagger out of his belt. He strolls over to Mans, he thumbs the edge of the dagger near Mans' throat.

SOLDIER Did the drunkard say something? I thought the drunkard made some remark.

HILD No, it's all right. Here, you're welcome to the eggs.

SOLDIER We'll be coming back this way soon. After we've dealt with the rats in the mill. We'll call in for a drop of that marvellous ale of yours, ma'am, that can make a man so brave first thing in the morning.

The troop hesitates at the edge of the ploughed land.

SOLDIER Go round by the hill. Earl Magnus gave strict orders. We're not to go through the cornfields.

LIEUTENANT Never mind that. This is the nearest way to the mill.

The soldiers cross the field
One of them strums an instrument.
They sing.

I wish I was far from here,
I wish I was home in bed,
Pretty Ragn in my arms,
A jug of ale at my head.

MANS *angrily to Hild* You had no right to tell them I was drunk. There's not enough malt left to make a mouse drunk.

HILD I had to tell them something. Remember what happened to Glum in Orphir. He hid his bacon and bread from them. They hanged him from his own rafters. And Skop, they drowned him in the millpond for keeping his wife from them.

MANS *to his scarecrow* Mister Scarecrow, I have something to say to you. You've been frightening the rooks all month. I want to put in a word for them poor rooks. It isn't much they take, is it? A seed here and a grain there. It's the six-legged things made in God's image that I hate, the horsemen. They eat up everything. They rape and rob wherever the fancy takes them. I doubt you and me, Mister Scarecrow, can do nothing about the horsemen.

HILD *pulling Mans' coat* Hurry, Mans. There's more horsemen down there, at Sabiston. And the mill, look, there's torches all round it.

Mans and Hild begin to hurry back to their house. Two figures appear against the sky.

25

MANS Here's two more of them.

HILD That's only Jock and Mary. She's half blind. They harm nobody, poor things.

Hild finds her black hen and puts it in her apron.

HILD Here she is, the hen! So this is where you hide. I'm going to keep you in a box beside the fire, chookie.

Mans and Hild go out. Jock and Mary come down from the hill, going on to the shore.

MARY What are all them shapes and shadows on the road?

JOCK Horsemen. Scottish soldiers, Norwegians. They're all over the place.

MARY *stopping before the scarecrow* This one must be the sergeant, he's standing that straight . . . Sergeant, have you such a thing as a ha'penny, sergeant, for a poor blind woman?

JOCK That's a scarecrow.

MARY Reduce him in the ranks, Jock. His coat's better than the one you have on.

Jock strips the hat and coat from the scarecrow. The tinkers go out.
A flame shakes out from the besieged mill at the shore. Scattered silvery cries fuse into one red yell of rage and terror and exultation – it is as if the very soil of Orkney was in bitter travail . . .
Enter the Man with the Parchment.

THE MAN WITH THE PARCHMENT 'People of Revay, for that there have been grievous losses by slaughter and wounding of those loyal to Earl Hakon Paulson, true and sole and only EARL of ORKNEY, TAKE NOTICE that after harvest there will be a GENERAL CONSCRIPTION within the bounds of this parish of BIRSAY, of all able-bodied males betwixt the ages of 16 and 40, to bear arms in defence of their liege lord the said EARL HAKON PAULSON, and of His Majesty of Norway.

26

Scene 5 PRELUDE TO THE INVOCATION OF THE DOVE

CHORUS
A few months pass – a time for nails to be forged, thorns to be woven, vinegar brewed.

In Norway the king goes north to the ice, after walrus.

In Orkney, red earl and black earl are powerless; the wounded chessmen seek their own disordered places.

The islands are full of widows.

The monks in a green holm celebrate, in a surge of sorrow, the passion of Christ. They wear long black coats.

The peasants have broken the last barley crust.

Five men stand at the door of Christ Church in Birsay. They wait in two groups: Havard – Sighvat – Sigurd, and Hold – Finn. The first group wear predominantly black clothes, the second red. They are not at the moment, clearly, on speaking terms (though they look across the gulf at each other from time to time with hope and expectation and suspicion).

Havard Gunison knocks at the church door.

Far inside, the monks are singing a fragment of a Passiontide psalm: 'Thou hast moved the earth, O Lord, and thou has shaken it. Heal its wounds, for it is breaking up . . .'

The tinker woman Mary has found her way into the church.

A young monk comes and sets palm branches on the altar.

Havard knocks again, louder.

Brother Colomb opens the door.

BROTHER COLOMB What's all this? Battering on the door like that, in Passion Week!

HAVARD It's very urgent. We must see the bishop.

BROTHER COLOMB I don't know if his grace can see you. I doubt if he even *wants* to see you. Wait here.

HAVARD We couldn't get across earlier for the tide.

Brother Colomb goes out.

SIGHVAT I told you. We're not welcome.

MARY *under a statue* My eyes are worse than ever they were, Lady.

SIGURD *to Havard and Sighvat* Listen to that. The same chant over and over again. You'd think they'd get tired of it.

HOLD *to Finn* Nothing ever changes here. It's exactly the same as when we were schoolboys.

SIGHVAT *to Havard and Sigurd* I don't like it. We shouldn't have come here in the first place. The less the church has to do with this the better.

SIGURD We *had* to come. The bishop is a landowner too. He's one of us.

HAVARD We must be unanimous. To leave the church out would weaken our hand.

SIGHVAT I don't like it. I know the church. The priests will end by taking charge of the whole affair.

Enter Bishop William of Orkney.

BISHOP God be with you, strangers.

LANDOWNERS *a ragged response* And with your grace.

BISHOP What brings all our former students back to Birsay? On such a cold morning too.

They all start to speak together.

FINN This trouble in the islands . . .

HOLD You're a landowner like us and . . .

SIGHVAT Remember, the church is not to interfere . . .

HAVARD Hakon and Magnus, they're . . .

The bishop holds up his hand for silence.

MARY I wandered off the road this morning, Lady. I fell in the ditch. That never happened before.

BISHOP Please. What do you want? I take it you haven't come to make a retreat.

HAVARD Father, we represent the landowners here in Orkney.

BISHOP Is that so? You haven't exactly got richer in the last year or two. You're welcome to Birsay all the same . . . Sighvat, your feet are wet again. You never learned to walk on the stones properly.

Well, and what does the gentry of Orkney want with the church?

Another discordant chorus.

HAVARD The earls, they're ruining us . . .

HOLD You're a landowner too, Father, and . . .

SIGHVAT We've banded together, all of us . . .

FINN Though we don't always see eye to eye, still . . .

SIGURD It's not as a priest that we need you in with us, but . . .

BISHOP *holding up his hand* Please.

MARY I'm frightened, Lady.

BISHOP The men of Babel would have built higher with a bit of mutual understanding.

Havard, you will speak on behalf of the others.

This war in Orkney – that's what you've come about, is it? *They nod their heads* Havard, Sigurd, Sighvat, you're in Earl Hakon's party. Finn, Hold, I know Earl Magnus is your man. Well, that's something. You haven't been keeping company this long while.

LANDOWNERS No, Father.

BISHOP *a flash of anger* You won't have come here to receive my congratulations.

HAVARD Father, we want peace.

BISHOP Do you? This is something new. Peace. For years it has been sword and fire with you. Son against father. Brother against brother. The crofter at harvest worse off than the rats in his barn. Here in Birsay our little hospital is full of wounds. The brothers hardly have time to pray.

MARY Who took my sight from me? I'd like to know that.

BISHOP The business of a community *is* peace. The crofter at his furrow. The fisherman at his creels. The monk at his prayers. The shepherd with the new lambs. The weaver at his loom. The merchant sending out a ship. The woman at her hearth, well, cupboard. The tinker on the road.

29

This peace is the heavy woven coat-of-state. The earl wears it. But it ought to warm and hallow and protect all the people. Rightly so; for it can be said that the whole community has worked at the weaving of it.

MONKS *chanting* '. . . My heart was prepared for disgrace and misery. I hoped that someone would weep with me, but there was no one.'

BISHOP It is a precarious thing at the best of times, this peace. Fishermen fight with shepherds in the alehouse on a Saturday night. The merchants squabble like gulls over every cargo out of Norway. There are differences at the well and the bleach-green.

Even here, in this church, where we live according to another kind of peace, you should hear Brother Fergus shouting at the choristers when they sing a wrong note.

Here and there a thread is always working loose.

We're all men, sons of Adam. There is an element in us – some evil instinct – that wants always to return to nakedness and savagery.

SIGHVAT We haven't come here for a sermon. We know what we're about.

FINN Just come in with us, Father. That's all.

BISHOP Havard, I am speaking to *you*. We must be clear about what we want. If there are crossed threads at the beginning, in the end the loom will be in total disarray.

HAVARD My lord, say what you have to say.

BISHOP I said the civil peace, under the earl, is always a chancy thing. Never yet in history has the harmonious city been built – however wise and good and strong the ruler was.

How must things be, then, when there are *two* rulers in a state? Two men with different natures, different outlooks, different appetites. And behind them a king who encourages their quarrels, the better to enforce his own supremacy.

You're tangled in a situation of great difficulty. No doubt about that. God knows how this thing is to be resolved.

I confess, speaking for myself, I have no idea. But if I can do anything to help . . .

HAVARD Father, we want you to join us.

SIGHVAT As a landowner only.

BISHOP Why?

HAVARD To force peace on the two earls, before they ruin us all.

BISHOP Havard, you can't *force* peace on a situation. All you can do is hold the door open and invite peace to enter.

SIGURD *impatiently* Will you join us, or won't you?

BISHOP I'm a priest, not a politician. I can ask the dove to fall on your counsels.

SIGHVAT Yes, all right, it's better without the church.

BISHOP Tell me, what do you intend doing?

HAVARD This, Father. On Easter Monday we have arranged for Earl Hakon and Earl Magnus to meet in the island of Egilsay –

BISHOP In Egilsay. The church island. On Easter Monday. Yes. Well?

HAVARD There will be a peace conference. The earls will go to Egilsay with eight ships each.

HOLD *Two* ships.

SIGURD Eight.

FINN I thought the number was two.

SIGHVAT No, eight.

HAVARD That matter hasn't been decided yet. It's of no importance anyway.

BISHOP One small fishing boat would hold you all.

HAVARD Father, they're *earls*. The occasion is important. It calls for some ceremony.

BISHOP Go on.

HAVARD We hope that the old wound will be healed there for good. Hakon and Magnus will meet face to face. That hasn't happened for years. The differences between them will be fully and frankly discussed. All the cards will be on the table. A peace treaty will be signed, with us – the landowners of Orkney – as guarantors. With frankness on both sides nothing but good can come out of the confrontation.

SIGURD We, not the earls, will be in charge of the situation. The earls have had their say long enough.

MONKS *singing* 'I sought someone to comfort me but found no one.'

BISHOP Here in Birsay we will pray for the dove to fall.

HAVARD *a little impatiently* What dove, Father?

BISHOP A splash of white against the darkness of the storm. A branch across the beak, brought we think from the tree of innocence and atonement. A simple blessing on the things that men propose.

Be sure it's the right kind of peace that you make. To make peace, the 'pax Christi', is to weave the seamless garment. But to make peace as politicians understand it – that is simply to patch an old scarecrow over and over again.

MARY *groping her way out of the church* I must be a fool, right enough, wasting my breath on a stone.

HAVARD Then you won't join us, Father?

BISHOP No.

SIGURD In that case we should go now, before the tide comes in.

SIGHVAT I don't want my feet wet again. I catch cold very easily.

BISHOP God be with you all.

Brother Colomb appears at the door, from inside.

He is carrying a basin of water and a towel.

The landowners file out under his pedantic eye.

BISHOP There's still time. The tinkers are taking whelks from a pool. That old woman is very blind now.

BROTHER COLOMB Father, it's Maundy Thursday. The twelve poor men are at the door. You must wash their feet.

BISHOP I think their treaty won't do much good at all, Colomb. For a month it will – perhaps for ten years. Then it's back with them to the old mischief again. What is desperately needed in Orkney this Easter is something more in the nature of a sacrifice: the true immaculate death of the dove.

The bishop and Brother Colomb go in.

The monks sing '. . . and they gave me gall to eat and vinegar to quench my thirst.'

The young monk returns with a black cloth which he drapes over the crucifix. He puts out the candles one by one. The monks sing on with deepening sorrow into the darkness of Good Friday.

Scene 6 THE KILLING

CHORUS

A few days pass. It is Good Friday. Christ has died on a skull-shaped hill. The earth is a stone.

The king kneels in a gold-and-ivory chapel.

The earls point ten ships at the kirk island – two ships like doves, eight hurtling hawks.

Women sit in the churches with covered heads. Their Lord is laid in a heart of stone.

The monks in a green holm sing with stiff lips a seven-fold threnody. Black their coats.

The earth is a stone.

The sea above many stones is a barren fishless tremor.

Darkness in the small kirk of Egilsay. It is the lowest ebb of time. A priest's voice recites the Entombment:

They took the body of Jesus . . . And bound it in linen cloths . . . With the spices . . . As the manner of the Jews is to bury . . . There was in the place where he was crucified a garden . . . And in the garden a new sepulchre . . . Wherein no man had yet been laid . . . There they laid Jesus.

Into the midnight of Saturday a boy bears the paschal candle. We can see the women of Egilsay beside the crucifix: their faces smitten with new light, with springtime, with a never-more-expected hardly-yet-to-be-believed resurgence of flesh and spirit.

PRIEST

Rise up, my love, my fair one, and come away.

For lo, the winter is past,

The rain is over and gone,

The flowers appear on the earth,

The time of the singing of birds is come,

And the voice of the turtle is heard in the land . . .

33

During this reading a man enters the church. He kneels a little apart from the women. The light falls brokenly on his face: desperation, uncertainty, outrage, fear, doubt, shift and mingle under a cold mask.

The stage slowly lightens with the dawn of Easter Monday 1117. Two men with red coats stand on the highest point of Egilsay, and look to the north east. They are Hold Ragnarson and Finn Thorkelson, Earl Magnus's two chief councillors.

On the far hidden shore of Egilsay there is a sudden outcry and clash of steel.

WOMEN OF EGILSAY What is happening in Egilsay this Easter morning?
That is not the sound of the men going out with oxen.
It is not the sound of boats in the noust.
We are here today to be folded
In the heart of Easter, in the light of the new lilies.
A stranger has come to our kirk.
There is death upon him
As if he brought a skull among our candles.
The island outside is shaken with steel.
Who is this stranger?
There is salt at his mouth.
Look at his coat, woven with hawks and longships.
This Easter Monday our hearts are troubled.
But even so
We will be quiet, we will keep watch and ward
Among the candles and lilies
Here in the kirk, here in the looms of light.

The light comes welling up the east over the island.

A man down at the shore is lighting a fire.

There are a pot and a ladle and a joint of meat on the rock. He is Lifolf, Earl Hakon's cook. Jock and Mary stand watching him.

LIFOLF I have nothing for you. I told you. You've no business to be in Egilsay today. I'm Lifolf, Earl Hakon's cook. The place is swarming with gentry. Go on, now, get away. I have no time to

bother with the likes of you. The two earls are here, Hakon and
Magnus. I have to cook their lordships' dinner . . . Well then, if you
come back in the afternoon there might be a marrow-bone left, or
something.

The tinkers go out, Mary (whose eyes are two scabs now) holding Jock by the elbow.

*Earl Hakon Paulson and eight of his men (led by Sigurd and Sighvat) come up from
another part of the shore. The eight clash swords on shields. Earl Hakon remains silent;
he has been gathered into a web of plotting and violence not of his making. The Hakon
faction gather about a stone in the middle of the island. Hold and Finn move towards
them. They are met with a loud clash of swords.*

HOLD This is not the agreement, Earl Hakon.

FINN You have come to Egilsay with eight ships, not two.

THE EIGHT *clashing their swords* Where is Magnus?

HOLD You have brought a hundred bullies and brawlers to Egilsay,
not twenty men of peace.

FINN This was not the promise, Earl Hakon.

THE EIGHT Where is Magnus? *Sword-clash* Where is Magnus?

FINN Magnus is on the hill with his hawk.

SIGURD No. The sky is empty.

HOLD Magnus is down at the burn with his line.

SIGHVAT There's no trout on the rock.

Silence.

FINN As a matter of fact, Magnus is not in Egilsay today. He's no
fool, Magnus. He knew from the start he was dealing with cheats
and liars. He decided to bide at home. He is spending Easter
Monday at his mother's house in Holm.

THE EIGHT

Where is Magnus? *Sword-clash*

Where is Magnus? *Sword-clash*

Where is Magnus?

HOLD Supposing Magnus was here, what would you do with him,
Hakon?

THE EIGHT We will kill him.

FINN Earl Hakon Paulson, I'm speaking to you, not to this rabble of
drunkards. What, supposing Magnus was here, do you intend for
him?

THE EIGHT Death.

EARL HAKON *to his men* Be quiet. You're worse than yokels in a beer
tent. Finn and Hold have asked sensible questions. I will answer
them sensibly.

The swords clash.

EARL HAKON I have no ill feelings towards Magnus Erlendson.
Magnus is my cousin. I admire Magnus in many ways. He has this
sweetness, goodness, charity in his life – I wish to God there were
more men like him in the north. Listen, all of you . . .

To his own men

Stop that hellish babble! Put your swords away. Remember what
day it is, Easter Monday . . . I have given long anxious thought to this
problem of the divided rule here in Orkney. I won't hide it from you,
Finn and Hold – the violent removal of Magnus has been suggested
to me. But, in my experience, violence begets worse violence.
There's no *need* for violence at all. Listen carefully to what I have to
say. As you know, both Magnus and myself have mutual kinsmen in
Scotland: men of power, men who wish nothing but well to us both.
Now listen. I'm arranging for Earl Magnus to be sent to a friendly
castle in Scotland, somewhere in the Lothians or the Cheviots. In
the gardens and halls there, Magnus will be secure and happy. He
will be a kind of free prisoner. From then on I will be the sole ruler
of Orkney. I assure you of this, the king of Norway will never again
be able to interfere in our affairs . . . Magnus, of course, if he wants
to, can go on calling himself earl of Orkney – it will be a kind of
honorary title. But I alone, Earl Hakon Paulson, will wear that
coat-of-state.

*One of Earl Hakon's men, the standard-bearer Ofeig, is carrying the coat-of-state across his
arms: a heavy heraldic black-and-red- and-gold vestment, a thick sewn splendour.*

SIGURD No, Hakon, Magnus will not be going to Scotland.

36

THE EIGHT *chanting* **Magnus will die!**

The swords clash.

SIGHVAT We've heard all that kind of talk before. Earl Hakon, you disappoint me – I expected you to apply a bit of realism to the situation. We know all about the famous friends in Scotland. How the king of Scotland would love it, to have Magnus in his power! He would use Magnus, over and over again, to stir up trouble in Caithness and the islands. The king of Norway, the king of Scotland – there's no difference. This sickening business would go smouldering on into the next generation. You know that as well as we do.

HOLD Earl Hakon Paulson, I am not speaking to the liar and trouble-maker Sighvat Sokk. I'm not speaking to the red-faced louts behind him. I am speaking to you, as man to man. I see you're well aware of the character of your cousin. Such grace and goodness are rare things in any man. When they appear in a ruler they are to be treasured, surely. I'm asking you, therefore, what are you going to do with this jewel that you have in your hand? Are you going to throw it to these animals?

EARL HAKON I'm not a killer. My hands are clean. If I kill a man I kill him in the fire of battle, cleanly. My friend Sighvat has spoken his mind: there is, unfortunately, a lot of truth in what he says. Magnus could be used against the peace of Orkney, over and over again, if he went into the free Scottish exile that I mentioned (I was not entirely serious). It would certainly not work out in practice. But listen to this. Another solution occurred to me, only today, on our way here to Egilsay. I am glad now to be able to put it before you all. The plan seems to me to have no flaw in it. It is perfect in every way. It is a God-sent solution.

SIGURD Earl Hakon, please listen to me. We agreed, before we came to Egilsay, that the time for words is past and that the time for action has come. We agreed as to the nature of the action. Orkney's sickness will be cured by a lancing – a single swift stroke of the axe.

FINN We are listening to *you*, Earl Hakon. We are paying no attention to the filth and dung who are supposed to be your advisers. Speak on.

EARL HAKON I am going to put an image before you. I see my cousin Earl Magnus on a ship bound for Jerusalem. This voyage is what Magnus has longed for all his life. I see him praying for the folk of Orkney in the holy places. I see him walking along the fourteen Stations of The Cross, for our peace. I see him in Rome, receiving a blessing on behalf of all Orkney – and God knows we need it – from our holy father the Pope. Then I see Magnus . . .

SIGHVAT I have a holy vision of Magnus too. I see him stretched out with one candle on each side of his death-wound.

HOLD Be quiet, you trash. Your earl is speaking.

EARL HAKON I see Magnus's ship bound again for Ireland. Strangers welcome him at the harbour steps. In Dublin, a horse is waiting for our pilgrim. Westwards the horsemen escort him. They go among green places and quiet waters. I see a lonely arch, among rocks and breakers in the west. Hands like doves receive him there. Earl Magnus Erlendson of Orkney stoops under the arch. And that is the end of him. That is his death to this world. He will never be heard of again. A man with another name is taken by the brothers to a cell. There he will bide for ever, a prisoner of God. He will eat simple things, bread and honey and fish. From that stone will rise a fountain of perpetual beseechment for Orkney and its folk. We need have no fear of Magnus any more. It is the kind of life he has yearned for since his boyhood. Most important of all, there will be no filthying of our hands with murder and sacrilege.

SIGURD We thought we had a great falcon with us in Egilsay today, not a sparrow.

SIGHVAT *to the eight* Men, remind Earl Hakon Paulson of what we have come here for.

THE EIGHT *yelling and clashing their swords* The death of Magnus!

SIGURD We know well enough where Magnus is. He's skulking in the church there.

SIGHVAT That won't save him. We'll drag him out if need be.

Hakon – his imagination broken – turns and acts coldly and authoritatively: what has

to be done will be done with the least palaver and delay. He turns first to his
standard-bearer Ofeig, the bearer of the coat-of-state.

EARL HAKON Ofeig.

OFEIG I'm here, Earl Hakon.

EARL HAKON Ofeig, I want a word with you. I want you to do
something for me. I have a high regard for you, Ofeig. We've been
in a dozen battles and sieges together. You've always carried my
standard well. That kind of service merits a reward. Your day has
come, Ofeig. I'm going to do you the best honour I know. Take my axe.

Ofeig spreads the coat-of-state on the stone.

He takes the axe from Earl Hakon.

You will kill Earl Magnus Erlendson with that axe as soon as he
comes out of the church.

Ofeig looks at the axe, then at the church door, then at Hakon. He sends the axe crashing
into the dust.

OFEIG Do your own filthy work!

Earl Hakon stoops, picks up the axe, wipes some mud from the heft, and offers it slowly
round the eight. There are different reactions – some turn away, some shake their heads,
others wear stone masks. Not a hand reaches out to take the axe.

EARL HAKON Finn and Hold, I didn't expect this. They've ordered
their dinner and now they can't face it.

He goes to the side where the fire is twinkling among the rocks, under the grill and the
soup pot

Lifolf! Lifolf the cook! Leave your fires for a minute. Come here.

Enter Lifolf, aproned, carrying a ladle with gravy dripping from it.

LIFOLF Dinner won't be ready for an hour yet, my lord. The
broth's only just come to the boil.

EARL HAKON Never mind dinner, Lifolf. These gentlemen
indicating his company – they won't be eating today. Their guts are
queasy already . . . Lifolf, have you ever killed an ox?

LIFOLF I'm a cook, lord, not a butcher. I did kill a lamb once. That
was a long time ago, in the snow, poor thing.

EARL HAKON There's a lamb coming here now, in a few minutes.
You must kill him, Lifolf, with this axe.

LIFOLF I think I could manage that.

The Women of Egilsay turn and face the men round the stone.

WOMEN OF EGILSAY
We ask you to leave our island, Hakon.
We are poor people.
We have our corn to sow.
This is the time of the plough with us,
A busy season.
You are choking the glebe with swords and axes.
My lord, leave us alone.
We must open Egilsay now to the rain and sun.

Earl Magnus in the church goes up to the crucifix and genuflects.

WOMEN OF EGILSAY
Earl Magnus is not here.
Magnus has had his fill of wrangling with beasts.
His talk is with angels now.
Leave us in peace.
There has been enough, surely, of blood and sorrow.
If a certain man is under our arch,
That is nothing to you, Earl Hakon.
Whatever is in the church belongs to God.

Earl Magnus comes out of the church.

The sun is on Earl Magnus' face.

*Earl Hakon's men acclaim his coming with a frenzy of swords. Earl Magnus stands in
full sunlight. The women of Egilsay turn to him.*

WOMEN OF EGILSAY
Go back to the kirk, Earl Magnus.
They dare not defile the sanctuary.

Soon they must sail back to their women and wars,
Their farms and ships and ledgers.
Till then, beloved
We will bring you bread and fish and milk to the kirk,
Yes, and a coat to warm you.

Earl Magnus breaks the ring of women. He stands between the church and the stone in the middle of the field.

EARL MAGNUS Welcome, Hakon. I'm late. It's time the red seal was on the parchment.

LIFOLF *beseeching* Let me go back to my pots, Earl Hakon.

EARL HAKON *thrusting the axe in Lifolf's hands* There's no fame in making soup. You will do as I say.

Earl Magnus takes off his coat. He offers it to Lifolf.

EARL MAGNUS Take this coat, Lifolf. Feel it, man – it's good stuff. I wore it at falconry. I liked to wear it playing chess, too, and listening to the saga men. There's another coat somewhere. But maybe it's not for me, that coat. There's too much blood and ashes on my hands. That coat is woven of prayers, charities, vows, penances, fastings.
For a whole lifetime the shuttles fly.
The kindly ones should be here with that coat, now.
It lies in the loom, fold upon fold of light.
Lifolf, I'm bidden to a marriage-feast.
Will you open the King's door for me?
That axe is the key.
I wish they would hurry. The shining ones should be here now.
The shuttle is silent.
I dare not go naked into those ecstasies.

Magnus lifts from the stone the heavy coat-of-state.

EARL MAGNUS This other coat is for Hakon. He will wear it like a good prince. It never sat well on my shoulders. I did wrong to claim a share in it. What use is half a coat?
   This is a mystical garment too. It warms and protects all the folk

of Orkney. I think Hakon will wear it with justice and wisdom. The strong man who relishes government, only he can suffer it on his shoulders.

But Earl Hakon will not accept the coat-of-state. He will have in fact no further part in this shambles. He stands apart from the others, half turned away. Finn and Hold take the coat-of-state from Magnus.

Earl Magnus kisses the axe.

EARL MAGNUS Don't shake like that, Lifolf. You need a steady hand to turn this key. I can hear the wedding music inside the Hall. The feast has begun.

Earl Magnus puts his right hand to his forehead; there Lifolf must strike. The ring of peace-makers begins to close round.

EARL MAGNUS It's very cold here, outside.

The ceremony is joined by two old tinkers, who are wondering most of all – seeing they are excluded always from the goings-on of those in authority and even of those bound to the wheel of agriculture – why Lifolf is so long away from the fires and the marrow-bone he promised them.

EARL MAGNUS   I want my body to be buried in the kirk of Birsay. *He turns. He touches Mary on the face.* You come and see me there, dear, when things get very bad for you.

He kneels down beside the rock.

Hurry, Lifolf. They're half way through the wedding hymn. *He crosses himself.* In nomine Patris et Filii et Spiritus Sancti.

The witnesses gather round, hiding Magnus and Lifolf. There is a flash in the sunlight. The wind of the falling axe shakes the skirts of the beholders. The world is jolted. A single drop of blood falls on the coat-of-state.

THE PEACE MAKERS Amen.
WOMEN OF EGILSAY
The first spring rain has fallen.
Earth drinks it with joy.

Magnus has taken the first furrow in his brow.
He could not wait
For the flush of braird on our tilth,
The tossing cornstalks,
The sickles aflash in the russet sun.
Fare well, beloved.
The lord of the feast has welcomed you at the door.
The bread is broken inside.
The jars of wine are set on the long tables.
He goes among the harps in a fold of light.
Magnus is lost
In lucencies deeper than corn or dew or diamond.
Our eyes of dust can see no further.
This is enough. We have been too long from the hearthstones.
I will bake a loaf.
The fishermen will soon be in from the west.

Finn and Hold lay the coat-of-state on the shoulders of Earl Hakon: who seems now not to be aware of anything, hardly of his own existence. But in his pain and solitude he draws the collar of the magnificent garment about his throat.

The peace-makers move away from the stone.

The prone body of Earl Magnus is seen to be clothed in white.

Scene 7 HARVEST

CHORUS

The stone is split! A thousand beards thrust into the sun, they shout in the wind.

The king sits in Bergen, a silent golden chessman.

Hakon alone wears the sundered coat in the west: 'he became a good earl, a mighty chief, the Orkneymen desired to have no other ruler than Hakon . . .'

A croft woman bends to the scythe. The bronze waves fall.

The monks in a green holm sing a litany of saints. A new name is not yet gathered into that web. The voices go up and down – a monotony endless as the sea in the west. They wear the long bright coats.

The poor are abroad on the hill. A woman goes into her house. She returns with a loaf and a fish. She offers them in her doorway.

Jock and Blind Mary are on the road. By hills, lochs, crofts, peatbogs, fishing boats, howes, hamlets, kirks, wells they go all the year round, from leaf-and-lamb, into the bronze of harvest, and into white and dark winter, and beyond it into a new light.

They are old. The road is longer and sorer than ever they have known it. Mary clings to the tail of Jock's coat. She blunders and complains behind him.

MARY What's at the end of this road?

JOCK The Birsay kirk.

MARY A kirk? What are we going to a kirk for? There's nothing to eat in a kirk. O no, I'm going to no kirk, I can assure you of that. Kirk, indeed.

JOCK Come on, then.

They trudge on.

MARY I smell fish.

JOCK The Hamnavoe boats. They're in from the west.

44

They arrive at Hamnavoe, a cluster of boats and gray houses at the edge of shifting water.

Seven fishermen with a net at a pier. They are putting their catch in separate boxes, uttering a slow chant to ease the monotony of the work.

FIRST FISHERMAN *A fish for the king.*
SECOND FISHERMAN *A fish for the kirk.*
THIRD FISHERMAN *A fish for the earl.*
FOURTH FISHERMAN *A fish for the laird.*
MARY *interrupting* A fish for the hungry.
FIRST FISHERMAN *to Mary* Watch out!
MARY *going deliberately among boxes, nets, and fishermen's arms* A cod head for
a poor blind wife. We have a long way to go. My man's bad to me.
FIFTH FISHERMAN Give her a crab, for God's sake. Get rid of
them. *The fishermen give Mary a crab*
SIXTH FISHERMAN *A fish for the king.*
SEVENTH FISHERMAN *A fish for the kirk.*
FIRST FISHERMAN *A fish for the earl.*
SECOND FISHERMAN *A fish for the laird.*
THIRD FISHERMAN *A fish for the yawl.*
FOURTH FISHERMAN *A fish for the pot.*
FIFTH FISHERMAN *A fish in the chimney smoke, for a winter hunger.*

Jock and Mary leave the silver heaps behind.

MARY I got a hook in my finger. *She sucks a drop of blood* One small crab
– the mean brutes.
To the crab Don't snap your claw at me, hunchback.
To Jock You take him. *Jock puts the crab in his bag*
They trudge on.
MARY Ah, my poor feet!
JOCK It's all right. We're half road there.
MARY Where?
JOCK The Birsay kirk.
MARY *stopping* I'm going to no Birsay kirk. You can go to the Birsay
kirk if you want to. Say Birsay kirk again and I'll batter you – so help

45

me God I will. Leave me at the first ale-house door. *They move on one after the other*
There'll be a time to go to the Birsay kirk, yes, and the Birsay kirkyard too, when we're cold and rotten.

They trudge on. The round hills of Stromness and Sandwick stand about them.

JOCK Dark hills we're among, Miffia, Kringlafiold, Meeran-Bloo.
MARY I know. I can feel the shadows. *Cocking her head* I hear a cluck-cluck-clucking in the ditch.
JOCK A white hen. *He takes Mary by the arm and hurries her on* No more thieving. We're pilgrims. We need clean hands and clean hearts for the thing we're going to do today.

Mary shakes free from Jock. She makes coaxing noises, stooping down and beckoning with her forefinger. Then suddenly she jerks out her hand, grasps the chicken, and twists its neck.

MARY There, sweetness. You won't be feared of the dog again. No, nor the hawk in the cloud either. *She gives the chicken to Jock to put in his bag*
JOCK You've made a small snow-storm in the ditch. Hurry on. God forgive our thieving. *He crosses himself*

They trudge on, many a mile. Mary drags at Jock's coat-tail, the breath harsh on her lip.

MARY Jock.
JOCK What now?
MARY Don't go so fast. What's your hurry? Stop till I get my breath.
JOCK We're going up Revay Hill, a steep place.
MARY *she stops and listens* What's Revay whispering about? – whisper, whisper, whisper. I never heard such gossip.
JOCK The sickle in the oats. Harvesters all over the hill. A good crop too. Stooks as bright as trumpets.

They are climbing up Revay Hill, a heavy fertile wedge thrust into the surging blue and white of the sky.

Mans and Hild and other harvesters are sitting in the shade of a wall eating their mid-day bannocks and cheese, and passing the ale jar. The sickles lean against the wall.

MARY *whining* A bit of bread for an old blind wife. A bottle of ale to wash it down.

MANS Them bloody tinkers again! *He shouts to his dog* Seize them, Bran! Take them, boy! See them off.

A dog barks among the oats. The farmer threatens Jock and Mary with his sickle.

JOCK *backing off* We're just going. I'm sorry, sir. We won't trouble you at all. *As the farmer still advances on him he produces a club from inside his coat* Only don't push me too far . . . *In a panic* Do you see this club? You bloody ignorant yokel, don't thwart me, look at it, it's splashed red! It's scarlet with the blood of slaughtered men!

MARY *screeching* Crush him, Jock!

JOCK Six battles I've been in. I stood where thousands fell.

A HARVESTER Was that the time you shook your shirt? *The harvesters laugh*

MANS *advancing with raised sickle* I'll cut you to ribbons, you trash!

HILD *coming between them* Think shame, Mans. We were poor as them last winter. And poorer the winter before that. *Her basket, brimming with food and flagons, is under a stook in the shade. She takes a bannock and a bottle from it* The war's over. We can all eat in peace.

We have Hakon, our good earl, to thank for that. We're only as rich as the poorest folk among us. Here's something to put in your mouths.

She gives the bannock and ale to Mary.

MARY *feeling the gift* I've seen thicker bannocks.

JOCK Thank you, lady.

MANS *to the harvesters* Come on. The whole field must be cut before dark.

THE HARVESTERS *returning to their reaping with a chant*
Seven loaves –
The laird gets one.
The earl gets two.
The king gets three.
The seventh loaf,
That's for the peasant,

He must share it with God and the birds.

Jock and Mary trudge on, one after the other, silhouettes against the west.

MARY It's cold all of a sudden.

JOCK The sun's down.

MARY There's a good fire in the ale-house. It's the thought of that that's kept my feet going all day, the fire and the ale and somebody talking sense for a change. There might be a fiddle.

A man in the ditch, with an empty sleeve and a pin leg. We might just recognize the lieutenant who violated the cornfield in Scene 4.

MARY *holding her nose* What a stink at the crossroads!

JOCK It's that old soldier with one arm and one leg.

SOLDIER Please, a bite, friends.

MARY Out of the way, you rag-bag.

SOLDIER Pity, kind lady.

MARY Don't 'kind lady' me. *She feels his face with her hand* Your face is a bunch of thistles. What stone did the likes of you crawl from under?

SOLDIER I fought in the war, lady. The first winter I fought for Magnus. I got broken with horses' hooves – that's the way I lost my arm.

JOCK What happened to your poor leg, mister?

SOLDIER An axe, man. Just a bit of a scratch along the thigh. That was the second winter. I was on Hakon's side that time. My leg turned purple. In the end they sawed it off.

MARY Serves you right. No more war dances for you, mister. *She spits* Horsemen – what trouble they caused for a year or two!

Come on, Jock.

SOLDIER I haven't eaten for three days.

JOCK *to Mary* Give him a bit of bread.

MARY No. The scum that he is. He'll think twice before he puts on a helmet again.

JOCK *offering the crab to the soldier* Here then, take this crab.

MARY *snatching the crab back and putting it under her shawl* Nothing for murderers.

They trudge on into the twilight.

MARY War's a good thing for blacksmiths.

JOCK Yes, and girls and grave-diggers.

MARY I'm smelling the sea again.

JOCK We're going down into Birsay.

MARY There's a touch of silver in the air, a shiver.

JOCK The moon's out over the village, a thin white thing, Mary, like a girl the night before her wedding.

MARY Old beast.

JOCK I've watched the moon a thousand times. Changing, always changing, like a woman. First, this trembling bride. Then a beewife with a honeycomb. A few nights more and she's a red-faced washer-woman – she swills linen in the burn, bright shirts. Then she's a widow with a small candle.

MARY *sarcastic* Jock the poet.

JOCK In the end she's nothing but an old hag, a poor blind crone among the ashes. Then the black boards nailed over her face . . . *He crosses himself* Rack-curse-cat-end-patchy. *Jock's jargon for 'requiescat in pace'*

MARY So. *She sighs*

They are approaching the steep green tidal holm of Birsay, with its cathedral and cloister and palace.

JOCK Thank God the tide's out. We can cross over now.

MARY Where are we?

JOCK Never mind. Take both hands to the tail of my coat. We're on seaweed and slippery stones.

MARY *up to the ankle in sudden coldness* Ah!

JOCK Don't yell like that. The holy brothers'll hear you. You put your foot in a pool, that's all. Come on.

MARY The sea's on the one side of us and the sea's on the other side of us. We'll get drownded, Jock.

JOCK The tide's far out. Listen, kittiwakes in the crag, all sleepy.

MARY There's a seal splashing out there. Whistle to him. *She shrills with her mouth*

JOCK   Quiet. We must be quiet.

MARY   Is there an ale-house the place we're going?

JOCK   No.

MARY   *screaming* Ah-h-h-h!

JOCK   For God's sake! This is a place of silence.

MARY   A razor-fish. Are there any bits of toe on the rock? That slippery stuff's blood.

JOCK   It's seaweed. Take hold of my coat. Follow me. There's only one more pool . . . and a wet stone . . . and a few shells . . . and sand . . . and now we're on the island. Be quiet. The bishop doesn't like the kind of pilgrims he's getting lately. *He listens* Come on.

MARY   Where to? I won't go a step further till I know where we're going.

JOCK   I told you. We're going to the Birsay kirk.

MARY   *I'm not going to any kirk.*

JOCK   You must come.

MARY   *I will not.*

JOCK   Yes.

MARY   *No.*

A pause.

MARY   I'm tired of the holy talk of them brothers every time they put a bandage on my eyes. *O you poor afflicted one, bear your cross with patience* . . . I don't want any more of that kind of talk. O no. I've had my belly-full of that palaver.

JOCK   Stay where you are, then. Sit on the beach. I won't be that long . . . *He leaves Mary and goes up to the church* I'll have to hurry. They'll be starting their Matins soon . . .

He opens the heavy door cautiously, enters, dips his fingers in the holy water, crosses himself, genuflects to the altar, looks about him, and kneels down among the images, at a new tomb. The only light in the church is the hard ruby flame on the altar.

JOCK   Noble one, are you hearing me? I made a tin pail in Rackwick last night. I meant it for you. She sold it in a Hamnavoe pub for porter, Mary. She has a throat on her like a salt fish. Or more like a smouldering peat. Or more like a bit of the everlasting brimstone.

Listen.

Silence. The muted sound of the sea, still ebbing.

I'll tell you what I'm here about. I won't hide it from you any longer.
As if you didn't know my errand already. It's not me, it's that old
woman.

Silence.

I've saved this bit of candle for you. *He takes a candle from his pocket and lights
it from one of the church candles and dribbles hot grease on the tomb and sets his offering
up, a reeky flame* Beeswax. I'm trying hard to mind on a prayer. Light
for light, man. Ask the Lord to put a glimmer back in her skull.

MARY *outside, plaintive* How much longer do I have to bide out here in
the cold!

JOCK A small blink. She was as shining a lass as ever walked the
roads. You must have seen her in her best days, many a time, going
to the Dounby Market with pans and laces; among the ponies
and the fiddles. She could see in them days like a hawk through
crystal.

MARY *outside, hilarious* I've drunk half the ale. It's good stuff. I could
dance.

Silence.

JOCK I'm not blaming you for not listening to a tink.

Silence.

She's nothing now. A mouth on her like a warped purse. Two cold
stones for eyes. That's what Mary's come to. Just an old blind sack
of sins.

MARY *whimpering* Jock, it's midnight. A rat ran over my hand.

JOCK All right then, Magnus, say nothing. I was travelling through
Birsay anyway, for rags. I just came in out of the wind for a minute. It
isn't beeswax at all, this candle, it's whale tallow.

Silence.

I'll tell you what. I won't steal or swear any more. Tell the Lord God that. Truth. No lies from now on. Every morning and every night I'll say ten Hail Marys – beads of dew on a wild rose.

A thread of gray in the weave of night

MARY *Jock.*

Silence. The last glut of sea on a rock. It is full ebb.

JOCK Well, well, say nothing. Maybe it's all for the best. Folk take more pity on a blind person, you get a lot more ha'pennies on the road. There's more to spend in the pub at the end of the day.

More gray threads through the fabric of night, then a yellow thread . . . Jock turns to the sweetest statue in the cathedral.

Our Lady of The Seven Sorrows –

Bishop William enters.

BISHOP Who's that? . . . What are you wanting here? I couldn't sleep all night for the screaming of some old woman on the shore.

JOCK *in a humble voice, struggling to his feet* Your reverence, I was asking the saint to help us.

BISHOP The saint. What saint?

JOCK St Magnus.

BISHOP There's no St Magnus. You're wasting your time, my man. That's only the tomb of the earl who was murdered in Egilsay. You might as well pray to a stone. I'm getting a bit tired of telling that to all the poor things that come here. They're beginning to come now from as far away as Iceland and St Kilda – hare-lip and scab and consumption. Ugh!

JOCK I'm sorry, your reverence.

BISHOP *a little kinder* Whether this dead man is a saint or not is not for us to say. He might be. The authorities haven't decided yet. A man isn't a saint because all the tramps and comic-singers of the day think he is. When Rome says he's a saint, that'll be time enough for me and you to ask for his help. Do you follow me?

JOCK Yes, your reverence. Thank you.

It is dawn. The small flame of Jock's candle is lost in widening circles of brightness.

BISHOP Bless your faith, all the same. The brothers are coming in to sing their psalms. You'd better go now. You had no business to be on this island at all, do you know that? This is private property.

JOCK No, your reverence. Thank you. I won't come again.

The sea begins to turn round with a sound like a struck harp.

BISHOP The old woman's quiet now – she's sleeping under the rock, I think. You can cook your breakfast. Then off with the pair of you.

JOCK Yes, your reverence. Thank you. We'll do that.

BISHOP I'll remember you both in my Mass.

Jock bows himself backwards out of the church. Bishop William shuts the door. The monks file into the choir with lit candles and censers swinging and voices going up and down.

MONKS Kyrie eleison. Christe eleison. Kyrie eleison.

Mary wakens under the rock.

MARY *yawning and stretching herself* Is that you? It's high time.

JOCK *squatting down beside the fire on the beach: to Mary, very despondently* That old bishop, he drove me out of the church. Did you hear him?

MARY We should get a bob or two for the candle-sticks. Did you pinch the chalice too?

JOCK Shut up.

The monks begin to sing a Litany of the Saints of the North.

MONKS *Saint Olaf the king, pray for us.*

JOCK Is that all you left, the chicken neck?

MARY I had the queerest dream. Folk in a winter field, in the snow. They were all lamenting how poor they were. First was a merchant fat as a pig – one of his twelve ships was wrecked on Braga. A farmer then, girning – a rat was in his barn. Then a holy brother – 'O' cries he, 'I'm betrothed to the Lady Poverty' – and by God he looked it. Then – I never saw anything so queer – the king of Norway hung

53

with silks and diamonds – he comes arm-in-arm with that pin-leg horseman we passed yesterday on the road. The king and the tramp, they had one bone between them and they were gnawing at it like two dogs. Then they would leave off, and wail, and throw their arms round each other. They all stood in the snow in front of the kirk, and you were there in the kirk door, Jock, you and the bishop and a man I didn't know – a man with a red wound in his head.

JOCK There was too much badness in you. The saint couldn't do a thing about your eyes.

MONKS *Saint Ninian the traveller, pray for us.*

MARY Then the birds wakened me . . . Jock, I'm hungry again.

The sun has risen. Mary rises. She is ready for the road.

MARY Let's get away from here. I need a drink. Come on. The sea's throwing her arms about the place. We'll have to hurry.

Jock gets to his feet. A freshening wind throws the rising sea against the island.

MARY Hurry. I got spray on my face.

A wave breaks on a rock near Jock and Mary and cascades them with spray, or with a squandered treasury of opal-and-pearl-and-emerald (it depends how you look at it). The sources of light are troubled for a moment.

A glister of oil spills into the quenched lamp. Mary screeches. She puts her hands to her face.

MARY Ah-h-h-h! . . . . . . My face! Scum. You scratched me.

JOCK Nobody touched you.

MONKS *St Tredwell, keeper of eyes, pray for us.*

Mary whimpers. Then she is quiet. She plucks, tremulously, a flower from the grass.

MARY Daisies. *She kneels* And here's a seapink.

JOCK No more. I've had enough of you for one day.

MONKS *St Cormac the sailor, pray for us.*

MARY *getting to her feet, pointing* That's a plover . . . There's a teeack.

JOCK *stops eating and puts down his bone* It's a lark, Mary.

MARY That's what I said, a lark, I know a lark when I see one. *She looks at Jock* What's this face, like a scarecrow?

54

JOCK It's me you're looking at, Mary.

A pause.

MARY We must be making do. You had black curly hair last time I saw you. *She plucks a white hair out of her own head and looks at it and gives it to the wind* Age. Ashes. God keep me from pools. God keep me from stones that shine in the rain . . . Jock, will there be stars tonight? *She licks her finger and holds it up* I thought the wind was yellow at this time of year, harvest. Age. Time. *She begins to move off* I'm supposed to be grateful, am I? Well, I'm not. Can I get the dark years back again? One place I do want to see, the Birsay ale-house. It's sure to be open by this time . . . *She bends over the grass till her face shines like a woman at a milk-churn* Marigolds. That was a good name to give them. *She wanders off* The stones are awash. All right then, I'll find my own way across. Drown if you want to.

Mary goes out.

JOCK Who would think a ha'penny candle would light the world?
MONKS *St Columba of the islands, pray for us.*

Jock stamps out the fire. He goes up to the door of the church.

JOCK *shouting St Magnus the Martyr, pray for us* . . . Jock the tinker said it before any of you.

He takes his bundle in his hand and moves off after Mary.

THE WELL

Scene 1   THE KEEPER OF WATER

An island shore.
The Keeper of Water stands. She waits.

THE KEEPER OF WATER A new time. A new time in a barren
island, new creatures to complete the dance of bird and plant and
fish and wild boar, of fire and sweet water as yet unlocked.

A new folk has come to the island at the end of winter, with spade,
seedbag, ox, flint: after a hard voyage.

Impossible the tasks that face the wanderers. How will they find
shelter from the black storm and the thunder?

ISLANDER There are stones everywhere. We will build houses and
byres, first. I have said so. Gather stones.

THE KEEPER OF WATER How can they make little fields in the
total bog of this island?

ISLANDER We will dig. We will drain and dung. We will sweeten
the soil with sand. This I have said. Sink the spades deep.

THE KEEPER OF WATER How will they warm themselves, under
the cold boreal sun?

ISLANDER The hill – it's thick with good black peat. I have told
you. Tear fire from the bog.

THE KEEPER OF WATER Without water there is no life, no
continuance or renewal, no lucency in act or word or ceremony.

ISLANDER Look, a black cloud. It's kissing the hill-top! Turn your
faces to the rain.

THE KEEPER OF WATER The harps of the rain throbbed all night.
Rain silvered the island. Rain sank to the roots of the first corn.
Rain gathered in the burns and ran out into loch and sea.

Rain came, by secret ways, to a rock under the earth. And the
water sought the sun. A spade dug. Hands gathered beach stones.
The water shone in the light, in quick bright circles, on and over the
rock, into the brimming cups of their hands, through salt knuckles
and smoky fingers and palms dark from ox and furrow – a thousand
brilliant singing drops.

This is it, the new stone-girdled well.

The people will never lack for water, so long as there is an island in this place. So long as there is a well. So long as a raincloud, now and then, kisses the hilltop. So long as the people handle this gift of water with reverence.

Now the well is made, I give it into their keeping.

Scene 2 DRAGON MEN

Centuries later.

Three Celtic women stand at the well with wooden buckets.

FIRST WOMAN Yes, he did. I'm telling you. It's true. Bran saw the
strange ship this morning. It was black against the sun.

SECOND WOMAN Bran see things nobody else sees.

THIRD WOMAN No, but Glim saw the thing too. 'It's a monster,'
said Glim, 'not a ship. It has a head like a dragon. It has one big
square wing.'

SECOND WOMAN Put more water in your ale-kirns. Then your
men will see only fishing boats in the west – maybe a whale, now and
then, on the horizon. No dragons or mermaids.

THIRD WOMAN Glim isn't a liar. Glim was frightened when he
came in from the sea. The fish trembled in his hands.

SECOND WOMAN Well, what if there is a ship? I heard my
grandfather say, once there were three ships from far away, from
Atlantis. A long time ago. The sailors were friendly. The sailors
came ashore with apples and pieces of silver. The islanders gave
them a barrel of sea birds, salted. Then somebody struck a harp.
There was dancing round the well all day.

FIRST WOMAN Hurry. You talk too much. I want to get back to the
village. I'll carry my kirn and spinning wheel into the old broch. It's
half ruined but I think they can't touch us inside the broch.* We're
safe there.

SECOND WOMAN What was that? Listen.

THIRD WOMAN I hear nothing.

SECOND WOMAN I heard a cry among the hills. Breaking and
burning. Listen – a song!

[THE VIKINGS' SONG]
We give you fires.
(Give them the gift of fire.)

* Early Celtic fort or keep.

We Vikings
Are generous with our torches.
Your well is too far away
To kill our blaze.
What are your hearth-flames?
Small pot lickers.
Our fire is a terrible dragon.
Our fire will breach the broch wall.

The three buckets are brimming with water. The three faces turn towards the hills.

A stranger with a blond beard and an axe has come up from the shore. At first the women do not see him.

The stranger brings down his axe clanging on the stonework of the well. The island women turn. They cover their soundless mouths with their hands.

The stage darkens, but for a fire-glow here and there.

NORSEMAN   This island is ours. We are the men from east over sea, from Norway. The well, the broch, the hill, the shore, the caves, the cornfields, the women.

They are all ours.

Scene 3 BLESSINGS

Centuries on.

A girl with blond hair and an old woman at the well.

The girl dredges up a full bucket. She looks, gives a shrill cry and splashes the water out over the stones.

OLD WOMAN Tut! What are you doing? Wasting the good water.

GIRL There was a beetle in it.

OLD WOMAN What harm would a beetle do you?

GIRL I'm terrified of beasties.

OLD WOMAN If you'd seen the drought that was here one summer when I was a girl, you'd be more careful with water, if there were a hundred beasties in it. The precious water drops. You think, God help you, water's the plainest commonest thing in the world.

GIRL And so it is.

Three monks have come up from the shore. They stand with their buckets – their heads bowed, bald circles shining atop.

GIRL Oh no! – Look, granny, the bald-heads are here, monks. Let's get away, quick.

OLD WOMAN Wait. Listen.

FIRST MONK Bless fire – the red sun in the sky that ripens the crops, and warms us at the hearth in winter. It puts a circle of candle-light on the holy psalter when a voice reads to us in the refectory.

MONKS We bless the fire.

SECOND MONK Bless air – the fine wind of summer that tosses the barley, and the sea wind that brings peaceful ships from haven to haven. Bless the circles of sound in the air when the bell is struck at matins.

MONKS We bless the air.

THIRD MONK Bless earth – the hidden cells of clay that nourish the seed, and the green shoot, and the heavy yellow stalks of harvest.

Bless the bread that is pure nourishing earth-essence, the bread on the table. Bless above all the bread on the altar, 'panis angelicus'.

MONKS We bless the earth.

FIRST MONK Bless water. How should we merit this gift of water? It is so beautiful a thing, water, only the mind of God could have imagined it. It is the seven huge oceans, it is the single jewel of snow on the chancel window. It is the loch and the burn. It is the palace of fish. It is the cloud tangled on the hilltop. With joy and astonishment we lower our buckets into the well.

MONKS We bless the water.

The three monks lower their buckets.

The old woman and the girl stand aside, their buckets not yet filled.

THIRD MONK Brother Adrian.

SECOND MONK What is it, Brother?

THIRD MONK In my water-bucket there is a worm of a most repulsive aspect. Shall I decant water with worm, and dip again?

SECOND MONK Brother Sylvan, the worm has as much right as you to the gifts of God. Would you kill the worm with stone and drought? Put our brother worm, with reverence, in that little pool over there.

THIRD MONK Brother worm, live in the pool.

One after the other, the three monks take up their buckets and go, with not so much as a glance at the women.

GIRL What simpletons! I nearly laughed in their faces.

OLD WOMAN They know. They know what we have forgotten.

She dips her bucket.

Come up, blessing of water, if it's only to wash old Thorf's shirt in, when he comes up from the shore smelling of tang and limpets.

Scene 4   THE KING'S WELL

*Generations pass. In the fifteenth century Orkney is ceded by Denmark to Scotland as a
pledge for the dowry of the Danish princess who married James III.*

A soldier with a helmet, breastplate and lance is standing beside the well.

*Four women approach with buckets. They hesitate when they see the soldier. At last the
boldest one speaks.*

SIGRID Please, we want to draw water. Will you make way for us?

The soldier says nothing.

The women look at each other.

SIGRID I need water for brewing.

ASA Yes, I need water for washing doorstep and hearthstone.

LIV My man, he'll be coming in dirty from the ox and the plough.

SOLDIER This is the king's well. Keep back.

SIGRID This is everybody's well, mister! King's well, indeed. Folk
have been getting water here since the beginning of time.

SOLDIER This is King James's well. When your men pay the king's
taxes, and obey his laws, then the king will allow you to draw as
much water as you need. Until then, water from this well costs one
shilling a bucket.

INGERD King James! Who's King James? Our king is the old kind
wise king across the sea, in Norway.

ASA King Christian never charged a farthing for this water.

SOLDIER The price of the water is one shilling a bucket. Until a
certain word is spoken.

SIGRID Liv, there are four of us. We could take this Scotsman and
break every bone in his body.

LIV We could. We could grind him into grains.

SIGRID Mister, there's hundreds of heavy stones on the shore.
We're going to give you them for nothing, in the teeth.

SOLDIER I am the king's man. Beware.

*An islander enters, a ploughman with muddy boots. He stands watching. He has a little
bag in his hands.*

65

Slowly the women, taking up stones, approach the Scottish soldier.

The soldier's lance trembles. He turns uncertainly.

ISLANDER You women, stand back! Put down the stones.
    To the soldier The island men have had a meeting in the field. We've spoken together.
SOLDIER Well?
ISLANDER We will pay the tax to the king in Edinburgh.

The islander rings the little bag of coins like a bell.

SOLDIER I'm glad. I will take this word and this money to the earl in Kirkwall.
ISLANDER King James is our man from now on. There's no other way.
SOLDIER *to the women* King James of Scotland gives you his gracious permission to take water from his well – as much as you want, for nothing.
    God save the king!

The soldier with the tax money goes out one way.

The islander goes back to his plough and ox and furrows.

The women one after the other dip their buckets.

LIV King James's water! It's God's water, and the people's water.
ASA Yes, and it always will be.
SIGRID That Mansie of mine is a fool. They're all fools, the men. I'd have liked to do something bad to that foreign soldier.
INGERD Shush! What do we know about their politics? It's peace now. And that's the best. The water's free again.

66

Scene 5 FOREIGNER

Two girls at the shore, centuries on.

RACHEL When is it going to be, your wedding?

SONIA In May.

RACHEL Sonia, I know you'll be happy. You're a lucky lass.
Nobody's ever asked me to be his wife.

SONIA There's time enough, Rachel.

RACHEL Oh no. I'm twenty-three. Nobody's ever wanted to take
me home from the barn dances. I'm ugly. Every time I look into the
rockpool down there, the pool says, 'You're ugly, Rachel. You'll be
an old maid always'.

SONIA You have a pretty mouth.

RACHEL Nobody's ever wanted to kiss it. Never.

SONIA Look – a ship in the Sound!

RACHEL Oh, a lovely ship!

SONIA I don't like the look of her. She isn't one of our ships,
Rachel. I think she's a French ship!

RACHEL A French ship would never come so close.

SONIA Rachel, you wait here. I'll go to the big house, the laird. I'll
tell all the farms on the way.

Sonia leaves her bucket and runs out. Rachel is alone, with her plain earnest face.

RACHEL *to herself* Never bend over the rockpool, Rachel.
That water is bitter, bitter.

A foreign voice startles her.

SAILOR Pardon, pretty lady.

RACHEL Who are you? Go away. Please.

SAILOR Lady, I will tell you. We come from far away. The water in
our ship is rotten. Many sailors are sick. One has died. I have come
to buy water from your well. Look, silver coins. We are not
war-men. We are peaceful merchants.

RACHEL I can't sell you the water. It isn't mine.

SAILOR Where is the chief of the island? We need many barrels of water. I will pay him good gold.

He holds up a gold coin.

RACHEL Listen, sailor, you've been seen. The men will capture you if you bide here. They're on the way now.

SAILOR Such hard words from such a beautiful mouth.

RACHEL Don't make a fool of me. I'm ugly.

SAILOR You are the most beautiful girl I have seen since we left Brest.

RACHEL Here. Be quick. Take a drink from this bucket. No, I'll fill a cup for you. Hurry. I hear feet on the road. They'll kill you, man. Hurry.

The French sailor drinks greedily. And again. He gives the cup back to Rachel.

SAILOR But this does not cure the sickness of a whole ship.

He kisses Rachel, then turns and runs down to a small boat at the beach.

The factor and men from the farms come in, armed with sickles and flails.

FACTOR Rachel, thank God you're safe. That's a Frenchman out there. Some of the sailors have landed. Did you see any movement on the shore?

FIRST FARMER Down there – look! – a small boat.

SECOND FARMER It's leaving the shore. Two men in her, rowing.

RACHEL One of them was here. He spoke to me. He wanted water. I gave him a cup-ful.

FACTOR Was he armed, Rachel? Did he threaten you?

RACHEL No.

FIRST FARMER Let's see the money. How much did he pay you?

SECOND FARMER You're not supposed to give aid and comfort to an enemy.

FIRST FARMER Show us the silver piece he gave you.

RACHEL I gave a cup of water to a sick man. And the man, he . . .

FACTOR He did what?

RACHEL He made me feel like a princess.

The men laugh, all around Rachel. They point to her and laugh.

SECOND FARMER You a princess! . . . With that ugly face!

FACTOR *to Rachel* You might find yourself in trouble when the laird comes to hear of it.

Rachel puts down her bucket. Water spills from it. She covers her face.

FACTOR Get back to the hayfield. I must send word to Kirkwall at once.

Scene 6 SONG FOR A DAY TIME

Islanders at the summer well, waiting: a crofter, a farm wife, a girl and an old man.

GIRL Our rose bush – it's all shrivelled in the yard.

FARM-WIFE I never remember a summer like this one. Sun day after day for six weeks.

CROFTER The earth's cracked. The oats are only two inches high.

FARM-WIFE Yes, and they're gray with dust.

CROFTER The island's scorched, as if a dragon had breathed on it.

GIRL Our cow, Nell, she's dying of thirst. The horse is nothing but hide and bone.

FARM-WIFE No water for men and women, far less beasts.

GIRL The bees – they're the only happy ones this summer. Bees everywhere, hot and stinging.

FARM-WIFE How will we live next winter? The millwheel doesn't turn. There'll be no bread, no ale.

CROFTER What'll happen, old one? You've seen a few summers, wet and dry.

OLD MAN It always rains in the end. It'll rain till you cry for it to stop. It will that – I've seen it all before.

FARM-WIFE There's not a cloud to be seen.

CROFTER The sun's like a nail – a bronze beaten nail in the sky.

OLD MAN I saw a long worm in the ditch. 'Hello, worm,' said I. The worm sang, 'Look out. Rain's coming. Put your hats on.'

CHORUS
[SONG FOR A DRY TIME]
Cloud, come back to the hill.
The mill
Is silent, that used to be never still.
Burn, flow sweet from the hill.
The girl stands at the shore with an empty pail.
The old wife cannot swill
Shirts and shifts, and dry them on the wall.

70

Mansie has lacked all month his mug of ale.
Cloud, come back and kiss the burning hill.
Fill
With endless circles of song our ancient well,
Till the buckets drip and spill.
This summer only the seal and the whale
Splurge with a will,
Skarf and sillock and whirling gull,
And the rock-bound whelk . . .
GIRL Stop! A cold bee stung my face, here!
CHORUS *continuing*
. . . Let Nell our cow give butter and cheese and milk
And stroll like a queen through the heavy grass in a coat of silk.

The islanders hold out their hands.

ISLANDERS The rain! The rain!
FARM-WIFE Listen, deep down, the well's drinking.

Scene 7 INTERIM

The Keeper of the Well appears again.

KEEPER OF THE WELL Time here, in the island, is a single day, repeated over and over. The same people, dawn to sunset. The same things: birth, love, death. The old die, the children come dancing into time. Water shines on the new-born and the dead.

Now other ideas have drifted over, have rooted in the island. Time is no longer a single day rising and falling. Time is stretched out into the past. Time runs on into the future. And the island's past is seen as ignorance and savagery, dung and clay; the future is a golden road with treasures richer than gold at the end of it.

In the new school at the centre of the island, water is no longer a mysterious element, life-giver, brightener; it is H_2O.

The island is changing. The old ceremonies of the island are withering. There is no need for ceremony any more. Ceremony is the ignorant dance that holds us to the past. We must (they say) uproot ourselves, turn free faces to the future.

How shall the Keeper of the Well live in a place without ceremony? Can I stay and watch the withering of the well?

I think it is time for me to go. Perhaps, if I am needed, I may return, from the secret sources, from the dark hidden crystal pulse at the heart of the island.

Scene 8   THE DAY OF THE LONG LEAD PIPE

Three modern women at the well, for the last time.

MARILYN   This is the last time I trudge from end to end of the island for a pail of water.

RITA   Tomorrow, is it? Is tomorrow the day?

PAULETTE   Tomorrow. At 12 noon the island councillor, Mr Skerry, will turn the tap on in the kitchen of The Bu. The laird, the minister, the doctor, the schoolmaster, the engineer, they'll all be there. Out it'll gush, the water, piped and filtered from the new tank on the hill.

MARILYN   It is high time.

RITA   What'll come of this well?

PAULETTE   It won't be needed. It'll be a ruckle of stones. It'll fill with all the rubbish of the island.

MARILYN   A good thing, too. We could never depend on the well. Sometimes it dried up. Sometimes it tasted of roots and iron.

RITA   And yet, what things have happened around this well! A thousand years old it is, they say. Think of all the women who'd come here and meet and go away. Think of the gossip and the quarrels and the fun.

MARILYN   No more. We turn a tap in the kitchen, and that's that. Kettles full, tub full, bath brimming. No trouble.

RITA   I think there'll always be ghosts round the well. The folk are leaving the island so fast, soon there'll be nothing but gravestones and ghosts.

The stage darkens. The voice of Mr Skerry the island councillor:

'So, friends, we have reached today another milestone on the long road of Progress. Much of the drudgery is now removed from our days. I'm sure the women appreciate that. No more trek, three times a day and more, in all weathers, to the old well above the beach. No more aching arms, no more heavy splashing buckets. The old well has had its day. I declare the reservoir open. I turn on the tap . . .'

Applause.

The light goes up. The well is abandoned and half ruinous.

73

Scene 9 MASQUE

Four maskers, in different colours: red, black, white, and blue.

BLUE MASKER Call him. Call in the islander.

A young man, barefoot, stands among the masks.

BLACK MASKER You are the islander, the first and the last man. The island is yours. You will do with it what you want.

ISLANDER I have done.

RED MASKER How many doors have you opened, since you first came here?

ISLANDER Four doors.

WHITE MASKER What did you find, when you opened the first door?

ISLANDER Fire. The red keeper that opened the door to me said, 'Here are flames for your hearth, fires for the hill-dance in midsummer. Here are your lamps and candles' . . . The door has stood open ever since. I came and I went. At last I came thanklessly. The peat cuttings shrivelled on the hill.

RED MASKER There is a fire beyond the fire.

THE MASKERS There is a fire beyond flame and ashes.

BLUE MASKER What did you find at the second door?

ISLANDER A good presence. She welcomed me with a strong pure kiss. Water was bright on our fingers and mouths. Malt seethed in the circle of water before Yule . . . At last we shut the door of Water. Stones drifted over the source. And the Keeper of the Well went away.

WHITE MASKER There is water beyond water.

THE MASKERS There is water beyond thirst and drowning.

BLACK MASKER Did you knock for entry at the third door?

ISLANDER I did. The door of Wind opened. And there were winnowing fans to separate chaff from grain. There were sails, furled, waiting for a wind to blossom from west or south. I came and I went a thousand times to the fishing in the west.

74

Then there came engine and oil.

I turned my back on that presence.

BLUE MASKER There is an air beyond breath.

MASKERS There was a wind once that choked your first stone houses.

RED MASKER The fourth door. The fourth door, Earth. There you stood.

ISLANDER My plough was the key to that door. Out of that deep cupboard I took my bread and ale. I broke the circles of bread and ale with my wife and children. We sat at our table in peace, all winter. Many a winter, many a generation, many a century . . . Then the young ones scattered. They went away. The plough rusted against a wall.

BLACK MASKER There is earth beyond earth.

MASKERS There is the earth that keeps skull and worm and the sleeping Dragon.

Death. The end of bread and breath, the end of all your seekings, the end of your story. A skull under a broken stone.

WHITE MASKER Tell him, there is a fifth door to open.

BLUE MASKER Inside the fifth door is the treasure you have heard about.

BLACK MASKER Will you open the fifth door, man?

ISLANDER I don't know that door.

RED MASKER Will you open the fifth door?

ISLANDER I don't have the key.

WHITE MASKER We have the key. The key was forged long ago, when the first number was uttered and the first question asked. Here it is. Take it.

ISLANDER Leave me in peace. I'm content with what I have: the hearthstone, the barn, the creel, the sail.

BLUE MASKER Here is the door. Knock.

BLACK MASKER Your eyes have been set on this door for a hundred years and more. Science. Knowledge. Wealth. They're all there, through that door. Would you waste your intelligence on a few fields and a fishing boat?

ISLANDER Give me the key.

The islander opens the door.

MASKERS This is the end of the island. The story is told. Here is the end of dance and ceremony. He has wandered out of the circle where he was safe, into the labyrinth. At the heart of the labyrinth is the treasure. Round the treasure the Dragon lies, asleep.

And now the island is empty.

The stage is darkness. There are a few barren sea sounds.

Scene 10 VOYAGERS

A group of people sit on rocks beside the sea.

There is an old man (the Chronicler); a child; a cripple; a young woman; a man.

It seems that they are blind.

They sit as patient as the rocks.

CHRONICLER 'Fair the city. Long we abode in that good place, many a generation. "Who desireth to go out through the gates of the good city?" – "What man now would trust himself, outside the city, to endure like a beast the four elements?" None. For it went well with us in the city. We lacked nor food nor drink nor repose, nor mind's delectation. Our hands were like flowers. Beyond the gates, wilderness and rough stone.'

WOMAN We are blind. In the year of the Dragon, when the city burned, those with hands felt out their way to the four gates.

MAN We were of the city, but strangers to one another. We came together at the Gate of Water, by chance.

WOMAN We went outside. There was a kindling on our blank faces. The sun.

MAN Then we heard the music.

CHILD 'Follow,' the music said. 'I will take you out of the power of the Dragon. I will take you back to the good first place.'

CRIPPLE We did wrong to follow the music.

MAN The boy with the flute went before us. We followed. The wind blew against our faces, petals and dust.

WOMAN Sometimes we lost the music. Then the wind gave it back to us.

CHRONICLER 'In the city, our speech had long been purged of poetry. Who should dance? Out of sorrow, out of pain and labour, comes music and the dance and chant. The last harp was burnt at the Gate of Fire, long ago. After that, our minds were quiet as flowers.'

MAN Now there is no music. The boy has left us here, among rocks. There has been no music for days.

CRIPPLE I think there was no boy. There was no music. We have come all this way to die.

WOMAN There was a boy. Once, in the mountains, I fell. His hand lifted me up. It smelt of . . . how shall I say? . . . roots.

CRIPPLE A dream of death. Perhaps we are dead – ghosts in the wind.

CHILD I saw images in the music. *Plough and cornstalk . . . Peatfires . . . The sail, the wind, and the fish.* It said at last, and this music was the best of all, *Well of sweet water.*

CRIPPLE These things have no meaning.

CHRONICLER 'And a guardian stood at each of the four gates of the city, so that the citizens could sit in peace in their houses tall as lupins. And it was truly a golden city, like a hive of bees, brimming with sweetness and industry and brightness. Nor was there any winter in the city.'

A brief silence.

WOMAN Do you hear the new sounds? Not the music. Other sounds I have never heard – a splashing, a murmuring, boom and whisper, a thunder that never stops. Now near, now far. And cold sharp circles of sound in the air.

CRIPPLE It is all a dream. We will wake up soon. And that will be death.

CHILD The flute said, 'The sea. I will leave you here beside the sea. The journey is not over yet' . . . Then there was no more music, only the sea sounds.

MAN I went down there, among the sea sounds. My throat was burning.

WOMAN I remembered to bring a jar out of the city. It broke in the mountains.

MAN I drank out of a pool. Such bitterness! My mouth shook with coldness and pain.

CRIPPLE Listen for the dark ferryman. Listen for the splash of his oars.

CHRONICLER 'How long did we bide in the good city? Many generations. And the guardians at the four gates kept the city. And the rulers of the city were just; they held their own high counsels with the gods. Those judgements were beyond our understanding. Yet whispers broke upon our sleep. We heard forbidden music, in our dream-time. We heard this "The Dragon. The Dragon will eat the city and the temples and gardens. Tomorrow is the day of the Dragon." Men did not look at each other. Honey and bread were tasteless in the mouth. We looked: the four statues were fallen at the gates.'

The music.

MAN Listen!

CRIPPLE I hear nothing. Only the terrible sea sounds. We have heard about the sea. It rises. It covers mouths and eyes. It sings at last in the hollows of the skull.

WOMAN It's the boy and the flute. He's coming back.

CRIPPLE I'll close my ears to it. I can follow it no further.

MAN We *must* hear it. We must hear it to the end.

CHILD 'Island, Well, Girl,' the music is saying. 'Open your eyes,' the music is saying. 'Look.'

MAN Our eyes are scars. Scabs and scars.

CHILD *I can see*! The grayness out there. It falls white among the stones, singing, again and again.

WOMAN I see what I think is a bird – a white bird on the rock, another bird flying. Now many birds. My eyes are like two crystals.

CHILD A pink flower is growing out of the rock. Look.

MAN I can see my hands.

WOMAN What is that lump in the sea over there, far off?

CRIPPLE I see nothing. I hear nothing.

MAN Look. Cliffs. A hill and a cloud. A beach, shining. Ruined walls. A circle of stone above the shore.

WOMAN The island is lost in the gray cloud. The cloud has fallen on the sea. You are all ghosts in the cloud.

MAN I can see my hands – they're shining, dripping.

WOMAN A freshness in the mouth. Suddenly my mouth is wet and sweet.

CRIPPLE The sun!

MAN Between the sun and the cloud, look, an arc of colours.

WOMAN I see someone standing beside the stone circle. A girl – she's holding out her hands to us.

Between two fragments of flute song, across the multitudinous noises of the sea: a thin summons.

THE KEEPER OF THE WELL Welcome, voyagers.

THE VOYAGE OF SAINT BRANDON

This play is based on the Temple Classics edition edited by F. S. Ellis (London, 1900). It was originally printed in William Caxton's *The Golden Legend* of 1483.

Scene 1   POET AND ABBOT

BROTHER BRIAN *the scribe sits writing in the cell of a monastery in the west of Ireland. He reads what he has written.*

Brandon, the holy man, was a monk, and born in Ireland, and there he was abbot of a house wherein were a thousand monks, and there he had a full strait and holy life in great penance and abstinence, and he governed his monks virtuously. And then within short time after, there came to him a holy abbot that hight Birnius to visit him, and each of them was joyful of other.

The door of an abbey on the west coast of Ireland in the 6th century AD.

Inside the monks are at their Matins. The sun has not yet risen but the sky over the hills is red.

An old man with a battered harp comes along the road and halts at the gate of the abbey; he plucks a random note.

The doorkeeper Brother Tomas comes to the door.

DOORKEEPER What's that?

A few more random notes.

DOORKEEPER Be quiet, whoever you are. This is a place of silence. What do you want?

More harpstrokes.

DOORKEEPER Why don't you speak? Who are you at all?
BYRNE *singing*
My name it is Byrne the poet.
I am a mangy old dog.
But I'm setting out on a journey
To the shores of Tir-Nan-Og.
DOORKEEPER Stop that row! Nobody asked you to sing. We are here to forget worldly songs like that. Go away, now.

83

BYRNE *singing*
I'm tired of a withered life.
My grave is half dug.
Somebody else can lie there.
I'm off to Tir-Nan-Og.

DOORKEEPER Look here, Byrne, just be quiet and I'll bring you out a bite. Then you can be on your way.

BYRNE *singing*
My famous coat of song
Is worn to an old rag.
Weavings of light I'll wear
In the halls of Tir-Nan-Og.

DOORKEEPER You're a foolish old man, Byrne. Don't you know at all what abbey it is you're making a disturbance at?

BYRNE What does it matter? There's too many monks in Ireland nowadays and too few poets.

DOORKEEPER Brandon is the abbot here.

BYRNE Brandon, is it? That famous scholar. I knew Brandon well the day before yesterday. We were born under the same stars.

DOORKEEPER Brandon's famous all over Ireland and far beyond it. Brandon sits awake half the night. He writes by a candle flame.

BYRNE He'd have been better drinking in shebeens among the hills.

DOORKEEPER You're wicked, Byrne, as well as foolish. Great wisdom has come upon Brandon this last winter. Some of the monks say he's studying too much – he's lost touch with the things of the earth. That may be. But it's a wonder to hear the heavenly wisdom he utters in the chapel at sermon time.

BYRNE *singing*
Many a tall proud lady
Will shrink to a loathsome hag,
But Byrne will ride young for ever
Through the woods of Tir-Nan-Og

Enter Brandon the abbot.

BRANDON Brother Tomas!
DOORKEEPER Yes, Brandon.

84

BRANDON Who's kicking up that unholy row out there at this time of the morning? I can't hear myself thinking.

DOORKEEPER It's Byrne, that old drunken poet. He won't go away.

BRANDON *coming out of his cell in the heart of the abbey.*

Byrne, is it? Well now, I haven't seen Byrne, or heard him either, for many a year. God bless you, Byrne. When I was a young man, Brother Doorkeeper – in the days of my vanity, you understand – nothing gave me greater happiness than that harp of Byrne. It sang like an angel at every fair in Munster . . . O Byrne, Byrne, there's a pitiful change come over you, Byrne, since last I saw you! You're snowed under with age.

BYRNE You're not looking any younger yourself, Brandon. You have hands on you like withered leaves.

BRANDON Brother Tomas, tell them in the kitchen to put a bit of fish in the pot for Byrne. Make a place for him at the table. And pour out a jar of ale.

DOORKEEPER I will, Brandon.

The Doorkeeper goes in.

BRANDON Now then, Byrne, I'm pleased to see you, for the sake of the old times. That was a sweet gift of God you had, that voice.

BYRNE It's well cracked now, Brandon.

BRANDON Where have you been, Byrne, in the last fifty years and more?

BYRNE In jails and fairgrounds. I forget all the places. I've been as far as Byzantium.

BRANDON Now, Byrne, God bless you. Would you sing me a verse or two more?

BYRNE I will, Brandon, because it's you.
They called me 'the wonder of poets'.
Now it's all 'tramp' and 'rogue'.
I'll make immortal songs yet
In the fairs of Tir-Nan-Og.

Where is my voice like a lark?
Where is my dancing leg?

I'll find them again, and better,
In the taverns of Tir-Nan-Og.

The prince would give me silver.
The princess would fetch me a hug.
I abandon their fickle favours
To be ageless in Tir-Nan-Og.

BRANDON There's still beautiful sounds in this fading world.
Tir-Nan-Og – the old ones used to believe that, I remember.
Tir-Nan-Og was some place in the western sea. The folk that came
by chance to that shore, they were young forever.

BYRNE That's true, Brandon. I've been there. And I'm going back
again soon.

DOORKEEPER *calling* The fish is on the table.

BRANDON Byrne, dear friend, you'll sit beside me. Come in now.
You must be hungry. How many miles have you walked since
sunset?

Later the same day. Brandon and Brother Tomas the Doorkeeper.

BRANDON Brother Tomas.

DOORKEEPER Yes, Brandon.

BRANDON Has our visitor gone yet?

DOORKEEPER Who, Byrne? Yes, he went away after he'd licked his
plate. He took his stink and his rags with him. He never as much as
said, 'Thank you'.

BRANDON I'm not following you, Tomas.

DOORKEEPER It doesn't matter. I'll light a candle for you in your
cell. The sun's down. It's your time for study.

BRANDON Wasn't that a great honour, to have a famous abbot like
Birnius visiting us?

DOORKEEPER Who?

BRANDON Birnius. The abbot from Donegal. I never heard such a
remarkable story from the mouth of any man.

DOORKEEPER There was nobody here called Birnius – not today.
I'll cut a pen for you. I'll fill the inkwell.

86

BRANDON No no, Brother – never mind that. There's more important things. I was very much taken by that story of Abbot Birnius. How kind of him, coming all this way to tell me!

DOORKEEPER There's been nobody here today, Brandon, but that old vagabond of a poet.

BRANDON Such a wonderful thing to have happened! Abbot Birnius has just come back from The Island of the Blessed – the Earthly Paradise – the Land of the Young. I would never have believed it. He actually stood on the shore of the island, Brother – Birnius and his company of monks. There was no night there, no winter, no death. The trees were loaded with fruit always – no budding and no withering. And the stones at the roadside – Birnius said they were solid diamonds and rubies and emeralds. They met a young man who had the face of an angel. He told Birnius all about the island. 'Heaven,' he said in his immortal voice, 'is that island further on . . .' And sure enough Birnius and his monks could see an island further west, brighter than the sun itself. 'But no mortal foot can stand there,' said the young man, 'not this side of death. You must content yourself (said he) with being my guests for a time. Here everything the heart can desire is yours for the asking. This island is the place Adam and Eve dwelt in (said he) before God sent them into exile for their disobedience. When you get home to Ireland, Abbot Birnius, tell the people what you've seen. A winter or two more (he said) and you'll sicken and die. You won't be sorry, either, for the joys of the Island of the Blessed are nothing to the joys of that other island further west . . .' Now, Tomas, wasn't that a wonderful voyage that the abbot Birnius made?

DOORKEEPER Yes, Brandon. Will you be needing a new piece of parchment tonight?

BRANDON No, Brother – not tonight or any other night. I have more important things to do . . . Tell me now, would you like to sail to The Island of the Blessed? Surely you would. Not all the monks can come through. I think Birnius said he had seven monks in the ship with him . . . I can finish that commentary when I get home again.

DOORKEEPER Brandon, I think you should sit down beside the

fire. You're looking tired. You've been working too hard. There's been nobody at the abbey today but that old rhymer.

BRANDON I never felt better in my life. I never – not even as a young man – felt such longing!

DOORKEEPER Brandon, you have to finish your book *On the Kingdom of Heaven*. The colleges in France and Germany can hardly wait to read it. What did the abbot in Iona say about it? – 'the last best flower in a life of study and piety'.

BRANDON Dross. Wind. Vain speculation. Malachi can finish it for me. Malachi is much wiser than me in theological things. Birnius was away seven years, I think. We'll have to take plenty of provisions with us – cloth, water, fish, salt, apples. What's Brother Colm busy at these days in the boatyard? Wasn't Cormac a sailor before he came to be a monk here?

DOORKEEPER Brandon, you've never sailed further than Aran. There was no abbot here called Birnius. You dreamed it.

BRANDON Let me see. Fishing boats – Colm will have to forget about fishing boats. He must make one great ship, the biggest in the world. Let me see now. That'll take most of the winter ... A light I never saw before was in the eyes of that old seafarer. It was kind of him to come. His feet must have been sore. Did you give him a basin of water?

The monks begin to sing Evensong inside.

BRANDON Look at that sunset. Brother, that's where the island is – somewhere beyond that glory in the west. Imagine it, no plough, no sickle, no quernstone – the corn there is ripe for ever.

DOORKEEPER Come in now, Brandon. The air has an edge to it. I'll heat a bowl of wine for you.

BRANDON *sings softly*

Bairn bringeth to graybeard
Bitter bone and ghost.
A man is young for ever
In the Island of the Blest.

DOORKEEPER It's that old poet to blame. Byrne. It isn't the first time he's put madness on the folk of Ireland.

Scene 2 THE CREW

Brother Brian writes, then reads what he has written:

And then St Brandon proposed soon after for to seek that place by God's help, and anon began to purvey for a good ship and a strong, and victualled it for seven years.

The Abbot Brandon's study in the monastery. Brandon at his high desk. Brother Tomas and Brother Malachi the theologian at the door, whispering together.

MALACHI Something will have to be done. He's crazy. Poor Brandon.

Brandon sighs; he writes with difficulty on a piece of old skin.

BRANDON What it is to be old! I can hardly see the parchment.

MALACHI It's doing the monastery no good. Everybody's laughing at us. Voyage to paradise! Have you seen the boat, Tomas? It's the greatest joke in the west. That boat will never be launched.

TOMAS Will it not, Malachi?

MALACHI Brandon ought to be locked away, the poor man, for his own good.

BRANDON That I should have to make this voyage, at my time of life! All I wanted was to die in peace, fall like a leaf from a tree.

TOMAS Father Brandon, isn't it time you were in bed? You've been up all night. Listen, the first bird is singing his matins in the tree.

BRANDON Bed, Tomas? What way can I rest, with all this work to do? Provisioning, sea-charts, star-charts. A thousand monks, all begging to come on the voyage, and only room for twelve . . . Would you like to come, Tomas?

TOMAS Brandon, who'd keep the door?

BRANDON What's that shadow and whisper over there? It looked just now like Brother Malachi. Brother Malachi, famous scholar. I expect the Holy Father will make Malachi abbot here, once I'm gone.

MALACHI *whispering* Non sum dignus.

BRANDON Whispers and shadows. I'm old, Tomas – half-blind, half-deaf, surrounded with shadows and whispers. But the blue wind of March is blowing outside. I feel as eager as a boy. Listen to that bird singing! Liam will have to come – that boy has a tongue like a blackbird. He'll keep us young.

MALACHI Die, old man. Go in peace to God.

BRANDON Tomas, I've made a list of the crew. I've thought long and hard about it. Here are the names written. You are to summon them now, one after the other.

TOMAS I will, Brandon. *Tomas goes to the door and calls* Colm!

Colm enters at once.

BRANDON Colm, friend, you drew the plan of the ship. You watched her growing week after week. The heaven-seeker. You must come on the voyage, shipwright.

COLM Oh, I will that, Brandon. Thank you.

Colm bows and stands against the wall in the first glimmer of sun.

TOMAS *calling* Finn!

Finn comes in.

BRANDON Finn, you sat on a bench all winter sewing a hundred ox-hides together – the ship's hull. You will come on the voyage, tanner.

FINN Can I? Thank you, Brandon. I will.

Finn bows and joins Colm at the wall.

TOMAS Maurice!

Maurice enters.

BRANDON Maurice, that altar tapestry of yours – you had to leave off work on that beautiful thing to make a blank gray sail. Come with us on the voyage, weaver.

MAURICE I'll do that, Brandon. And gladly, too.

Maurice stands at the wall, in growing light, with Colm and Finn.

TOMAS Cormac!

Enter Cormac.

BRANDON Cormac, what were you before you came here to be a monk?

CORMAC I was a seaman, Brandon. I've sailed as far as Cornwall and Spain.

BRANDON Brother Cormac, will you steer this new ship for us? She's to go much further than Spain. Much further.

CORMAC I never thought, Brandon, I'd get the salt in my beard again. I'd sail anywhere with you, Father.

Cormac goes over to the sunlit wall.

TOMAS Liam!

Liam comes in.

BRANDON Liam is it? Liam, you are to sail with us. What were you once? A tinker. Do you miss the little fires in the ditches, do you miss the poached trout?

LIAM I miss them, Father. I'll miss the music in the choir, too. But I'll come, I will that, gladly.

Liam enters to growing pool of sunlight in the cell.

TOMAS This'll take all day. Eamon, candle-maker! Padraig, bee-keeper! Maurteen, fisherman! Michael, stonemason! Sean, brewer! Seamus, horseman! Timothy, fowler! Come.

Enter the summoned monks, one after the other.

BRANDON Little brothers, you're all to be sailors for the next year or two.

SEAMUS Brandon, I get seasick. I'd rather stay here and look after the horses.

BRANDON Yes, Seamus, the blue and the gray horses of the sea. You'll be good with them, I know.

SEAN What'll they do for their ale? I'm frightened of the sea.

BRANDON Yes, Sean, many a famous island to see. There's

somebody I've forgotten. Let me see. Brian. Brother Brian the scribe.

TOMAS *calling* Brian!

BRIAN *entering* I was waiting outside. I thought you might need me.

BRANDON What are you busy at, Brian?

BRIAN You know that, Brandon. For years I've been working on the annals of the monastery.

BRANDON Will you come, Brian? I want a word-man on the ship.

BRIAN If you need me, Father.

BRANDON That's all, brothers. We sail tomorrow, Ash Wednesday. Go now. Say a prayer or two in the chapel. I want to be alone, and silent, for a while. There's been too much talk today. My head's in a whirl. Close the door, Tomas, after you.

The monks go out. Brandon is alone with the one shadow in the corner.

BRANDON *singing softly*

A cargo of rags and chaff,
Bottle and bone and dust,
We'll trade for immortal diamond
In the Island of the Blessed.

MALACHI Brandon, a word with you, please.

BRANDON You've been there, in the shadow, for a long time, Malachi. I wondered when you would speak.

MALACHI I've been looking and listening.

BRANDON I said I wanted to be alone, Malachi.

MALACHI I'm hurt, Brandon. I'm deeply wounded.

BRANDON Tell me, my son.

MALACHI I think this abbey is none the poorer of having me.

BRANDON A treasure you are to the abbey, Malachi. A shining light. They come here from all over Europe to read your commentary on Jonah.

MALACHI You have chosen a crew for your voyage. Whom do you choose? A bunch of yokels with heather growing out of their ears. What do they know about paradise terrestrial or paradise celestial, or any other kind of paradise? Would they know it if they saw it? They know nothing but digging, ditching, fishing, spreading dung.

Last summer that boy Liam stood for a month in the cornfield, singing and scaring birds. He was a tinker before he came here. An ignorant tinker. You have put a sword through my spirit.

BRANDON Malachi, this voyage is going to be long and hard. What's needed are men with thick shoulders – men who do things with their hands. They need another kind of strength too – the strength of innocence. Malachi, your back is rounded with sitting over books in the library.

MALACHI Very well. I wish you and your innocents joy of the voyage.

BRANDON Malachi, come back. Come back, dear one. You are precious to me. I am afraid for you, if you come with us.

MALACHI I have heard enough.

BRANDON You can come, Malachi, if you truly think you have strength for the voyage.

MALACHI Strength! I have the strength of learning, scholarship, holy wisdom. Who in this place has more strength? The allegory of the voyage, the cipher, the hidden levels of significance – how could Liam and Colm and Patch ever read that? There must be a scholar on the ship.

BRANDON Where have I put that parchment? Malachi, I am writing your name down. Come out of the shadow. Stand over there in the sun. Let me see you.

He writes Malachi: scholar and sailor.

Scene 3   THE ISLAND OF THE DOG

BROTHER BRIAN *reads* On the morrow they were out of sight of any land. And forty days and forty nights they sailed west, and then they saw an island far from them, and they sailed thitherward as fast as they could . . . and at last by the purveyance of God they found a little haven and there went aland every one. And then suddenly came a fair hound, and fell down at the feet of St Brandon, and made him good cheer in his manner.

CORMAC Brandon, land ahead!

BRANDON Where? Where? I see nothing.

CORMAC To starboard – beyond that smirr of rain.

BRANDON Praise be! An island. The first place we've seen since we left Ireland.

A dog barks on the shore.

CORMAC Furl the sail! Lower the anchor!

BRANDON We'll go ashore now, one after the other.

SEAMUS I'll not be going. Look at the sharp teeth in that wolfhound. He'll tear us to pieces.

BRANDON How cold the water is! Up to our necks, bright circles. This dog, Seamus, is a messenger. He's trying to say something to us.

The dog barks ferociously.

SEAN Look out, Brandon. He'll have your hand off!

BRANDON Good creature – this is a kind welcome you've given us. What's that you say?

The dog barks.

Oh, is there indeed? Is that so? Well now, the Lord's looking after us well. I knew he would. It'll be fine to sleep in the soft beds you describe, after all that tossing on the sea – and the sickness – and the salt scabs.

The dog barks.

94

You're very lively, my friend.

MAURICE The dog's running away, Brandon, with his tail between his legs.

BRANDON It wants us to follow. Follow it up the beach. That dog – that heavenly messenger – has just been describing a fine hall in the middle of the island.

The dog barks.

COLM There's a building over there, right enough.

BRANDON There's not a king the length and breadth of Ireland has a palace like that hall.

CORMAC It looks like a broken-down farm to me.

The dog barks.

BRANDON There's a chamber in the hall, the dog says, with a long table down the middle of it, and fourteen chairs set in order, and silver plates – in the centre of the table the best of food and drink.

The dog barks.

Thank you, dog. I never heard a kinder invitation to eat. Come on in.

The monks stoop in, one after another, through a low lintel.

THE MONKS There's a few bits of bread on the table, right enough . . . A jug of ale, is it? . . . The fire's burning . . . Here's a pot of soup on the hook . . . But not a soul in sight.

MALACHI The explanation is obvious. The farmer and his people saw us coming. They took to the hills. They thought we must be pirates. They left the dog to guard this place.

BRANDON A rich table. A honeycomb with all the sun of summer oozing out of it. And salmon – what a prince of the sea! Wine like rubies and wine like crystal. Eels. Mushrooms. Truffles. This would stretch the nostrils of the Emperor Charlemagne himself.

The dog barks.

Don't rush at the board, brothers. You've been studying patience and ceremony more than a day, I think. Go round the table with crossed hands. Now sit down. We'll begin to eat in moderation. Thanks be to God. Yes, Padraig, I'll take a little of the white wine, and the tail bit of the salmon . . . Brother Eamon, what will you have – a slice of venison?

EAMON Yes, Brandon, thank you.

MALACHI Venison – it's a bone with a rag of meat on it. Rabbit.

BRANDON Now, Padraig, what can I help you to? Here's oysters.

MALACHI Winkles. Winkles.

BRANDON And here a sheep's heart. Truffles. Trout. I can recommend the broth – it's like unicorn's milk.

MARTIN Ugh! No, thank you, Brandon.

BRANDON The venison, then?

MARTIN It's only a bone. The dog might like it.

MICHAEL Where *is* that hound? It's still skulking around, a growl here and a growl there. I don't trust it.

BRANDON You're thinking, maybe, it's a wonder there's no people to be seen in this gorgeous hall – only ourselves.

LIAM There's hundreds of fleas.

SEAMUS Somebody must have set the table.

FINN That's true. A woman must have baked the bread and boiled the bones, and brewed.

The monks belch, high and low.

BRANDON Belching never makes beautiful music. Some of you have come perilously close to the sin of gluttony. Have you finished eating now?

THE MONKS Thanks be to God. Yes.

BRANDON This great hall is full of unseen presences. The meal has been prepared for us by blessed spirits. They knew we were coming. And they're not silent either. Just as we can't see them, because of our sins, so we can't hear the heavenly music of their conversation. It must be very beautiful.

Brandon inclines his ear. Music circles around it, whirls in, till Brandon cries out with joy.

Ah!

LIAM I have a pain in my guts too, Father.

BRANDON Our talk just now at the table was like trough-grunting swine. The music! Listen to the music.

The dog barks.

MAURICE What's the dog saying now, Brandon?

BRANDON He's saying, there's a dormitory beyond with fourteen fine silk beds in it. We're to go in and sleep now, he says. Then we'll be fresh for our voyage in the morning.

The dog barks.

The dog's wishing us good dreams . . . The same to you, noble hound.

The monks move in order into the dormitory.

COLM Cow dung and hay! This is the byre. The farmer's taken his old cow into the hills with him.

BRANDON What soft fragrant beds! Too good for the likes of us. How fortunate we are.

MALACHI I'm not sleeping here. Fleas and lice and rats. The farm folk might come back and cut our throats. I'll sit beside the fire all night.

Ow – you beast!

MAURICE What's wrong, Malachi?

MALACHI The dog has bitten my hand. It's bleeding.

The cowshed is presently filled with snores.

Scene 4 JASCOYNE

BROTHER BRIAN *reads* And then they sailed forth . . . and at the last they *went upon an island weening to them that they had been safe, and made thereon a fire for to dress their dinner, but St Brandon abode still in the ship, and when the fire was right hot and the meat nigh sodden, then this island began to move.*

BRANDON Bellies, bellies! You think of nothing but stuffing into guts.

Where are my lean and abstinent monks now?

Very well: here is an island. Very well; go ashore, you have my permission. Very well; you have sea birds to eat and a stew-pot and kindling. Light a fire.

What keeps you then?

SEAN It's as bare and smooth an island as ever I saw. Not a grassblade, not a flower. A round hump in the sea.

CORMAC Colm, throw the rope ladder over it.

COLM Now, one by one.

MAURICE Don't slip. Don't slip. Up. Up. Up, up.

MALACHI *opening his chart of the ocean* This is certainly the isle marked ROCKALL on the chart. 'It cometh barely and abruptly out of ocean, and flocks of birds wheel endlessly about it. In tempest it is a rock to be dreaded by shipmasters, for that many barks have wrecked upon it. Yet on peaceable days mariners may land there for water and eggs . . .' This place is undoubtedly Rockall.

BRANDON *from the ship* Thank you, Malachi. Whatever it is, light your fires. Stuff your sides.

LIAM Will you not dine with us, Father Brandon?

BRANDON I will not. I will sit in the ship. I will meditate on the virtue of abstinence.

MARTIN There's a fine cave on the steep face of the island.

MAURICE It looks to me like a big mouth.

SEAN There's two little blue pools, one on each side of the foreland.

MICHAEL The smell from the pot! – Ah!

98

LIAM If that pot was a fiddle, I'd dance to the tune of it.

COLM Blow up the fire, Liam. Make a good flame.

CORMAC I thought the island moved then.

MARTIN Islands don't move. We haven't got our land legs yet.

CORMAC The plates now, Seamus.

SEAMUS I'm coming.

Seamus staggers. With a clatter the plates fall into the sea.

SEAN The plates! Why have you flung the plates away, Seamus?

SEAMUS They flew from my arms like birds.

The island sings with the pain of fire. It snorts. It heaves. It shrugs the monks one by one into the sea, together with the stewpot and the fire.

MONKS Save us! Save us! . . . The island's alive.

MAURICE We're drowned.

BRANDON Take hold of the boat. Climb in. Thank God you all learned swimming in the sweet waters of Ireland. This way. The island's blowing fountains of water from its top.

CORMAC Help us aboard, Brandon.

BRANDON Come in, Liam. You'll soon dry in the wind. Come, Liam. Come, Seamus. Come, Cormac.

MAURICE Look at the island now! – it's sinking.

MARTIN It's sunk! It's only a whirl in the sea.

BRANDON Come aboard, Malachi. What a pity you burned your *Book of Beasts*. 'Fables', you said, 'lies, nonsense'. Did you never read in your bestiary about the great fish Jascoyne?

Come aboard, Tomas.

Such green shivering people!

Look, I've broken a biscuit. That'll take the chill out of your bones.

You're the first men that ever cooked their supper on a fish's back.

Be thankful Jascoyne didn't make his supper of you.

Oh, look at Jascoyne. Did you ever see such fountains? Did you ever see such thrashings in the sea?

Scene 5   THE PARADISE OF BIRDS

BROTHER BRIAN *reads And then anon they sailed west three days and three nights ere they saw any land, wherefore they were right heavy, but soon after, as God would, they saw a fair island . . . And anon they went on land . . . and they found a full fair well, and thereby stood a fair tree full of boughs, and on every bough sat a fair bird, and they sat so thick on the tree that unnethe any leaf of the tree might be seen. The number of them was so great, and they sang so merrily that it was a heavenly noise to hear, wherefore St Brandon kneeled down on his knees and wept for joy.*

The many sea sounds, mixed with a few human groans.

Morning brightens about the voyage.

BRANDON What gray faces, again! What a miserable bunch of Jonahs! What ails you? The storm's over.

LIAM I'm feeling seasick still, Brandon.

MALACHI I'll be plain with you, Brandon. I wish I'd never left Ireland. My books – my dear unfinished manuscripts.

CORMAC Water barrels are empty, Brandon.

MAURICE I'm like a pillar of salt with the thirst.

BRANDON Tell me, Malachi – what day is this?

MALACHI How should I know? I've lost all count of days and weeks. There's no calendar on the ship.

BRANDON Men should know Lent from Advent, and Pentecost from Lammas, by the spirit's fadings and flowerings. There's a brightness on men's faces and hands on certain days of the year.

You did well to be sad yesterday and the day before. First was Good Friday, when Our Lord hung dead on his tree. Then it was Holy Saturday, when he lay in the heart of a stone.

But today is Easter Day. You should be laughing and dancing on the deck, not hanging your heads like sick dogs.

CORMAC Land ahead, Brandon.

BRANDON How does it look, Colm, that land.

COLM There's a black wood. There's a host of rooks building their nests in the branches.

Bird calls mingle with the sound of breakers.

BRANDON Cast anchor, Cormac.

MAURICE God grant there's a water-spring somewhere.

MALACHI Blackness. Bleakness.

BRANDON Brave music. Listen to the birds of paradise. You go ashore first, Colm.

MALACHI Birds of paradise! They're crows, rooks, choughs. A horrible din! It sets my teeth on edge.

THE ROOKS Aaark . . . aaark . . .

COLM *calling from the shore* There's a spring under the black rock here.

BRANDON Well done, Colm. Float the barrels ashore, brothers. I wish I knew what those heavenly birds are singing about. I'm sure they have something to tell us. Liam, boy, carry me ashore on your back.

THE ROOKS Aaark . . . aaark . . .

COLM Brandon, the water's a bit brackish.

BRANDON Let me taste. Nonsense, Colm, it's like a very good wine. Little bits of leaf and peat in it, that's all. Fill the twelve barrels.

Sing on, birds. You know it's Easter Day, don't you? You're putting us all to shame with your happiness. Little Brothers, those birds with their bursting throats know secrets we've forgotten.

Put the bung tighter in that barrel, Tomas.

A bird flies down from a branch and sits on Brandon's shoulder.

ROOK Aaark . . . aaark . . .

BRANDON What did I tell you? – this bird is speaking to us. What a sweet-mouthed bird. I bless you, little brother bird.

TOMAS It wants your tuft of gray hair for its nest, Father.

Brandon clasps his hands.

BRANDON Lord, give me great humility, so that I can stoop in through the door of The House of Birds.

I think I'm becoming a bird myself! I feel feathers quivering about me. It seems I understand the roundness of an egg; I feel its throbbings. I'm lighter and brighter than the wind. I'm beginning to have a worm-hunger on me.

ROOK Father Brandon.

BRANDON I'm listening, bird. Speak.

ROOK You see all the birds in the branches here?

BRANDON Yes, I do – beautiful creatures.

ROOK Only an innocent old man like yourself would think us beautiful. We have black feathers and harsh voices.

BRANDON Brother bird, I take leave to differ with you. Nothing that has come from the hand of God is ugly – however different in form and hue and function. What is more perfect, an elephant or a flea? Neither. They both issued perfect from the hands of the Creator on the Fifth Day. Likewise a star and a shell. We should shout *Gloria* to every natural thing on the face of the earth. To me you are a gracious company of birds, beautiful beyond telling.

ROOK Listen carefully, Brandon. We weren't always birds. Once, long ago, we were a company of angels in heaven. Long, long ago, when Satan rebelled against the Lord with his terrible legions, we did not join in the rebellion, but on the other hand we did nothing to prevent it. We did not stand close about the threatened throne. In the end, as you know, the rebellion was defeated – Satan and his hosts were thrust down into the pit of hell. What would the Lord God do with us, who were neither hot nor cold, but only lukewarm? The Lord spat us out of his mouth – he transformed us into crows – he sent us down into exile in this bleak black island – he changed the heavenly music we had uttered formerly into croaks and quarks. We are rooks – the swart birds that nobody loves.

MALACHI How can Brandon suffer that hideous croaking in his ear!

BRANDON Brother bird, that was a marvellous story. There's nothing much I can tell you in return. We're just a ship-load of Irish monks in search of the Island of Paradise Terrestrial. We've been a year and more on the sea, and still we haven't come to the place. I'm an old man. I fear I might die before I get there. I fear I might be buried in the cold ocean, not in the green hills of Ireland.

MALACHI Can a man in his sane senses have a conversation with a bird?

BRANDON Tell me, bird, shall I see that island or not?

The bird puts a single croak in Brandon's ear.

BRANDON *clapping his hands* Bless you for that, brother bird! Oh, thank you.

To the other monks Don't you hear what the bird says? We'll certainly come to the Island of Heart's Desire. Isn't that wonderful news? And in the end we'll get home to Ireland. All except one. All except one.

FERGUS The bird does nothing but croak, Brandon.

BRANDON And tell me this, how long will the voyage last?

ROOK Aaark . . . aaark . . .

BRANDON *in dismay* Seven years! – As long as that. Oh, brothers, what an old dodderer I'll be by the time we see Ireland again.

MALACHI Old dodderer – he's that already.

BRANDON Have you anything else to tell me, brother bird?

ROOK Aaark . . . aaark . . .

BRANDON Is that so? Who would ever have thought it? *He crosses himself* Thy will be done. *To the monks* You heard what the angel-bird said. The voyage will last six more years. Every Easter we are to come to this island and celebrate the Resurrection with the birds. Won't that be delightful now? He told me this, too. There's an island ahead with a fine abbey in it and twenty-four monks. My friend here says we're to spend every Christmas in that abbey. I can think of nothing more delightful.

Six sea circles, and then we come to the Blessed Isle.

CORMAC Brandon, the sun's down. We should get back to the ship before it gets dark.

CROW Aaark . . . aaark . . .

BRANDON We'll sleep here. Surely we've all had enough of that ship. I think there was never any bedspread in any king's palace so

103

comfortable as the leaves here under the tree – no, nor any pillow softer than this moss.

I feel very happy today, brothers. That is the miracle of Easter. Every Easter I am whiter and frailer than I was the Easter before, and yet my heart is renewed inside me. I'm running with my friend Byrne the poet on the hills. *He shakes his head* Some of you are still looking miserable. I don't understand it. The Lord is risen.

FERGUS Oh, we're cold, cold.

ROOKS *shouting as the sun goes down* Aaark . . . aaark . . .

TOMAS Brandon, shall we sing Evensong among the trees?

Brandon is listening to the cacophony of the rooks.

BRANDON We don't need to, brother. The birds are singing Evensong for us. Such courtesy. Such holiness. I never heard the Easter psalms sung so sweet and true.

Gradually the cawing changes to the plainchant: Jubilate Deo, omnia terra, alleluia, *and fades*

It is morning. One by one the monks waken. One by one the crows waken and emit a few random croaks.

BRANDON *yawning* Well now, that's the best sleep I've had since we left Galway.

The croaks thicken till the whole island is black with noise.

CORMAC Please, Brandon, let's go back to the ship now.

TOMAS I never slept a wink.

MALACHI There was mention of an island with twenty-four monks. I can't wait to get there. I'm starved for intelligent rational conversation. Nothing here but the yattering of yokels and crows.

BRANDON We're to be here till Trinity Sunday. The birds have invited us to stay.

COLM Oh no! Trinity Sunday – that's eight weeks away.

MALACHI Blackness, bleakness. Yew-tree and bog and rook.

Black rook music.

BRANDON *severely* Be quiet. Have some respect for the Divine Office. The birds are singing Matins.

And indeed the croaking changes to the Psalm: 'Haec dies, quam fecit Dominus; exsultemus, et laetemur in ea.'

Scene 6 THE STORM

BROTHER BRIAN *reads And then St Brandon and his fellows sailed forth in the ocean, and soon after fell a great tempest on them in which they were greatly troubled long time, and sore forlaboured . . . wherefore all the monks were so weary of that trouble that they set little price by their lives.*

FIRST MONK Oh, the dog and the rat! The storm – a dog – has taken me into his jaw. It shakes me up and about in a wheel. I am a rat, a gray wretched flung torn thing.

SECOND MONK What is north, south, west, east? What's up, down, sideways? The horizon falls in on me. The horizon is nothing but sharp broken pieces.

THIRD MONK Our mouths are round holes. Our bellies are quaking caves. We are a heap of gulping fish.

FOURTH MONK Wonderful a storm: O yes, when a man lies curled and candle-lit in a cell, woven wool up to the chin. Not this, never this. Oh!

FIFTH MONK The ship is like the harp of Byrne the poet with the great rage on it, the time he was sent empty-handed from the king's door.

SIXTH MONK My beard sang suddenly with bees, stinging drops. The hull has gone among salt hives. Golden Bee-keeper, guard your honeycombs.

SEVENTH MONK Lovely the bird, in a high blue tower of wind, turning. O lovely the fish, turning in its crystal house. Lovely the wheel of all the creatures. I am this thing – broken feather, fish-bone – a beachcomber picks it up and throws it down, scunnered.

EIGHTH MONK The wheel has borne us into a black quarter: from sun, from silver mists, from the rose-of-morning. Cling to the rudder, helmsman. Make white knuckles. Pray. Hold the prow into the black welter.

NINTH MONK I am thrust among slime and spew and weed, the

way the Sligo taverner takes a drunk penniless man and whirls him out.

TENTH MONK An hour ago, I took a sudden turn against the beautiful creation. A spasm of unbelieving. Stars and limpets are equal, and ugly, and without meaning. Ugh!

MALACHI The sea is a book of flung pages, a fearsome scroll. We are signs and characters in the script. The scholar cannot tell a syllable or a letter in all the mad writing.

TWELFTH MONK O Brandon, father, let the gray bird out of its prison. Why do you say nothing? It's time now for the dove so seek the olive. Brandon, shake it, the sweet word, from your mouth.

BRANDON What am I, a pig-keeper in a pig shed?

Listen, brothers. Time, we think, has the figure of a wheel. The life of all living things is in the figure of a wheel. Our voyage is a wheel. It takes us from a beginning to an end, round in a circle: as the first little white snowdrop thrusts up from the last snow of winter. The wheel takes all creation from chaos to the station of ice and fire, to the stations of the tree, and the fish, and the bird, and the animal, and man, and (somewhere beyond our understanding) to the station of the angels. What was that storm? A puff of wind from nor-east, a few ragged waves, a rattle of hail. You are men, and men moreover with cowls, pilgrims. A little discomfort turns you back to the station of the beast that suffers without hope. Keep your eyes free and rinsed and forward-looking. Beyond every storm, beyond the last storm of death, we come to a place of brightness and peace: the angel-gate. How should we ever know such a place if we did not know a little suffering first? The wheel moves on and takes us with it.

MONKS Oh! Ah! My head! My stomach! Oh!

BRANDON There's an island out there. There's a sea-dazzle between the ship and the shore. Do I hear a song of water?

EAMON Who stays in Ireland? The fool, the dull man with dry feet, he is ignorant of the great stir in the world beyond. I want, after this, only a hut and a small cabbage patch, and a hive, and a trout stream.

BRANDON The storm is over, brothers.

LIAM Listen – the song of water in a well. There's a sweet sound, if ever there was one.

MONKS Ah my head! . . . Ah, my belly! . . . O beautiful blue sea, green hill. O, silence.

Scene 7 THE ABBEY OF SILENT MONKS

BROTHER BRIAN *reads By the purveyance of God they came at the last into a little haven, but it was so strait that unnethe the ship might come in, and after they came to an anchor, and anon the monks went to land. And when they had long walked about, at the last they found two fair wells, that one was fair and clear water, and that other was somewhat troubly and dank . . . And anon after came to them a fair old man with hoar hair, and welcomed them full meekly . . . and led them by many a fair well till they came to a fair abbey, where they were received with great honour and solemn procession with twenty-four monks, all in royal copes of cloth of gold and a royal cross was before them.*

Brandon and his monks have landed on the island with the abbey. Brandon and half the company have gone to find the abbey.

TOMAS Twenty-four monks in that abbey. We'll have a good Christmas in the abbey. Shelter. Chickens. Wine. Fire.

COLM If there *is* an abbey.

FERGUS I tell you what would be better than the best wine – a sup of sweet water. I have a salt scab in my mouth: here.

SEAN Brandon's gone to find the abbey. It's time he was back.

COLM Dip your hand in the well, here, Fergus. Drink.

FERGUS The water stinks. Ugh!

An old man enters mildly. When he sees the monks he is suddenly angry.

OLD MAN Hey, you! Get away from that well! This is private property. Oh no – not *monks*! How many? – seven. All right, drones, take as much water as you want. Not out of that well, you idiot! It's all chocked and rotten. This other well, over here, it has good water. Fill your bellies and get out. Fill a barrel. Is that your ship? Good. Sail away. There's no room for more monks on this island.

LIAM It's Christmas Eve, friend.

OLD MAN So you speak, do you? That's something. Christmas Eve – I don't care if it's the Day of Judgement. Just fill your barrel and clear out. I have two dozen monks to look after already. I'm not feeding seven more mouths, I can assure you of that.

FERGUS There's another seven of us, friend. They've gone to look for an abbey.

OLD MAN I hope they never find that ruckle, for their own sakes.

TOMAS Brandon. You must have heard of Brandon, the Irish abbot. We're his men.

OLD MAN How long are you staying?

TOMAS Brandon says, till Twelfth Night. Then we sail west again.

OLD MAN Well, I might just hold out till Twelfth Night, seeing it's Brandon. (Of course I've heard of Brandon.) But no longer than Twelfth Night, mind. There's no food. I haven't the strength.

COLM Thank you, friend.

OLD MAN It's a great shame. An old man like me having to dance attendance on two dozen young strong men. It's my oatfield that keeps them alive. They never do a stroke of work themselves. The poor creatures, they're too lazy even to speak. They never open their mouths. They even sing their psalms in silence. God knows what'll come of them when I'm no longer here. I won't last for ever. At least you bald-heads speak . . . Here I was, happy and hardworking on this island, when suddenly a few winters back they came in a ship from Ulster, twenty-four of them. So I thought, 'Fine. It's lonely here. They can bide in the barn for a day or two. They can say a prayer for my old Betsy that's dead twelve years. They'll have stories to tell, they'll be good company.' Good company! – they've never said a word to me from that day to this. Never so much as a thank-you for getting my barn to bide in. A month passed. A year passed. I could see then that they had no intention of going anywhere else. I was saddled with them for good. The poor creatures, half-starved, shivering with cold that first winter day, silent as stones – well, I couldn't have them dying on me, could I? I gave them some cabbages and baked a few bannocks for them. And I told them there was plenty of land for them to break out and plough. 'And you can cut down them trees,' I said, 'and make a fishing boat' . . . 'And here,' says I, 'are two wells of water, one for you and one for me' . . . 'You won't live in luxury', says I, 'but you won't starve' . . . You won't believe this, that I'm going to tell you – they've never stirred a finger to put a spade in the earth or get a bucket of water. They go about always with hands folded in sleeves and their eyes on the ground, silent, bald heads shining. And who feeds them? Who lights their fires? Who patches their coats? Who sweeps out the barn that's their chapel? Who has to make their candles and their tapers? I do. I'm their slave. I toil for them winter and summer. They never let on that I exist. Did you say there were another seven of you? It's going to be a busy Christmas, fourteen more mouths to feed. Where did you say Brandon's gone?

COLM Up to the abbey to greet the abbot.

OLD MAN I hope Brandon thinks he'll get an answer. He won't . . . Well, I can't stay here gossiping all day. I've got to light the candles in the cowshed – they can't even light their candles. (My old cowshed, that's their chapel.) Oh, my back! – it's all that driftwood I dragged out of the sea since Matins.

Don't take the water from that well, I said. That's the monks' well. This well here, it has good bright sweet water. I see to it.

Brandon stands outside the open door of the barn. The abbot stands on the threshold facing him.

Behind Brandon, six inquisitive nodding heads. Behind the abbot, twenty-three silent earth-tilted faces.

BRANDON God bless you, Father Abbot.

Silence.

MARTIN Father Abbot, we're very pleased to be here on your island. Especially after that storm. Did you feel the wind and rain here too?

Silence.

CORMAC What are they, ghosts or stones?

BRANDON Father Abbot, we've come from our abbey in Ireland. We sailed here in a ship. There she is down there. We're in search of the Land of the Ever-Young. We were told in the Island of Birds that we must spend Christmas here in your abbey.

So here we are.

Silence.

SEAMUS We'd have a merrier Christmas on the ship, Brandon. It's a poor-looking place, this.

BRANDON Father Abbot, for the love of God speak to us.

He is answered by a thread of music that rises, it seems, from the stones and waters of the island.

BRANDON Thank you, Father Abbot. Oh thank you. I never got a sweeter welcome anywhere.

MAURICE I heard nothing – not a syllable.

MARTIN He did take his hand out of his sleeve for a second. That was something.

BRANDON *to his six* Brothers, I want you to know that you're in the presence of very holy men indeed. They have taken a vow of perpetual silence. (We should be ashamed of our chattering and wrangling from morning to night.) The abbot of this beautiful convent has a lot of things to tell us in his own way.

CORMAC I heard nothing either.

MAURICE Ask him when we're going to get something to eat, Brandon.

BRANDON Father Abbot, these talkative monks of mine are a bit hungry. They had a long sea fast. The storm ruined our sea larder.

Another strand of music.

BRANDON Father Abbot, that is most generous of you.

SEAMUS What did he say, Brandon?

BRANDON He has invited us, with the crystal tongue of the spirit, to eat with him and his monks in the refectory. See, they're all fluttering their hands. White doves. The abbot wants us to sit at his long table. Go in then, in order, one by one. I'll come last.

Brandon's monks enter the barn.

MARTIN There's nothing on the table, so far.
MAURICE What hard seats! What a cold bare refectory!

Music.

BRANDON Father Abbot has just told me the most wonderful thing. Every day the Lord sends to this island an angel in the shape of an old man. This angel covers the table with the most delightful food imaginable, sweet to the body and sweet to the spirit. Not only food – the angel sees to all their wants, clothes and bedding, candles and fire. Nothing ever wears out, nothing is lost or thrown away. The hands of the ministering angel are forever overflowing with bounty. The angel will be here any moment now.

The old man and the seven other monks of Brandon, the lingerers by the well, arrive. The old man has a basket on his arm and a sack over his shoulder and a bucket of water in his hand.

OLD MAN Here they are, I told you, waiting for their grub. Come in, come in. Your reverence, you never told me you were having visitors over Christmas. I wouldn't have known a thing about it if I hadn't met these sea-voyagers down at the well. I've had a back-breaking afternoon, I can tell you, baking extra bread. They'd better not be here after Twelfth Night – there isn't enough meal to feed fourteen more mouths.

He sets the basket on the table.

There then, help yourselves, that's an oatcake each.

He empties the sack over the floor.

Here's as many cabbages as I can spare. Six.

He sets the bucket down.

And here's your water. All right, all right, I'll put the cabbages on to boil. (I told you, they can't even boil water.) I suppose I'd better go back to the well for another bucket. No peace. No rest. Why I do it I'll never know. Maybe it's to get old Betsy out of purgatory.

The music.

BRANDON Father Abbot's thanking God for all this food. He says that the Lord is going to send thirty-eight loaves every day while we're here, instead of twenty-four. So we can all be merry together at Christmas.

SEAN Merry on oatcakes and silence and cold water – I like that!

Music, quiet surge on surge.

LIAM He's very talkative now, the old man. Look at Brandon nodding and smiling to nothingness.

MALACHI The tongue of the spirit is going some. His mouth is as tight as a trap.

BRANDON Is that a fact, Father Abbot? So you're Irishmen like ourselves. Fancy that now.

TOMAS What is he saying, Brandon?

BRANDON Father Abbot here has been telling me that he and his monks come from the abbey of Saint Patrick in Ulster.

MALACHI Saint Patrick's – it's been a ruin for 200 years.

BRANDON Wonders will never cease, Father Abbot. I thank you on behalf of my brothers, the voyagers.

MAURICE What's he saying now, Brandon, without moving his mouth at all?

BRANDON Father Abbot has been explaining to me that the weather is always good in this island. Blue skies, blue seas, a kind sun.

FERGUS Listen to the rattle of hailstones on the roof!

SEAN There's draughts like swords everywhere.

BRANDON And they've never been sick since they came here – not one of them, not for a single day. They look like boys, don't they?

MARTIN They all look about a thousand years old to me.

COLM They have enough loose skin between them to bind a library of books.

MALACHI I hate raw cabbage worse than seaweed. Ugh!

Music, again.

BRANDON This is the greatest marvel of all, Father Abbot!

MALACHI What is his ancient tongueless beatitude saying now?

BRANDON You won't believe this, brothers. They have seven wax candles in their chapel next door, and these candles are lit before every Mass without one of the monks putting flint to steel. And the candles never waste, no matter how long or how often they're lit. The angel comes every day, and lights them and keeps them tall and bright and fragrant.

Music.

We will indeed, Father Abbot . . . Brothers, if you've finished gorging yourselves, Father Abbot wants us all to keep The Vigil of the Nativity with him and his company in the chapel.

Music.

Father Abbot wishes us to follow him into the chapel, one after the other. It's Christmas Eve, remember. The Lord is about to be born.

A procession into the barn-chapel: Abbot, the twenty-four, Brandon, the fourteen.

The old man puts down on the byre-refectory floor two buckets of water, blue icy tremblings.

OLD MAN That's the last water I'm fetching today. Where are they? In the barn. They can't start till I light the candles. *All right, I'm coming*! I can't be everywhere at once . . . Let me see now, that's a double ration of oats to be ground tomorrow . . . *Hold on, mutes, I'm coming, I said*. Here's the flint. Where have I put that steel? Tut, the candles are wearing low. Stumps. Time I was making a few more. It'll have to be after Christmas. Well then, you can start your Evensong anytime you like. Who'd have thought ten years ago there would ever be a Mass sung in my old barn? What would old Betsy say? Well, but when you come to think of it, the blessed Lord, he first came down to a broken old byre too, to be born. That was one Christmas midnight, a while ago. And he keeps coming down day after day in the form of bread, for ever and ever. I never cease to marvel at that. It makes all this hard work worth while. I wouldn't put up with that old mouthless abbot for a minute if he didn't do what he does do with the corn I harvest out there in the field. *You can start anytime you like, reverence, I said.* I suppose I'd better go and kneel among them. Oh, my old bones!

BRANDON   This is the greatest glory I ever saw at Christmas, an angel in the shape of an old man lighting candles here and there about the chapel.

The three kings are on their way. The ox and the ass are eating their fodder. One angel has left the choir that sang to the shepherds. There he is, a splendour, kneeling among us.

At the altar the abbot gives tongue for the first time, a unison of flesh and spirit, in the 'Gloria', the song of the starry ones on the first Christmas.

ABBOT   Gloria in excelsis Deo
　　　　　Et in terra pax . . .

Scene 8 A DAY AT SEA

BROTHER BRIAN *reads And often the monks, out of thankfulness for the purveyances of God, by which he provided for them meat and drink and repose on the ocean whereon they sailed; and moreover out of thankfulness that God delivered them from many great and terrible dangers, sang litanies and hymns of praise, that it was a joy to hear on the peaceful waters.*

HELMSMAN Sunrise. Turn the hourglass, light-and-darkness. Monks stir. They kneel. Matins.

MONKS A wakening between dark waves.
      A white bird,
        Wings wide, scatterings of light.

HELMSMAN Gannets fishing. First fall of sand in the glass. They break fast, a circle of broken barley.

MONKS The birds, salt hungerers,
      Whirl
      Round the flung earth-dark crusts.

HELMSMAN Lauds. A shower from south. Wet sleeves.

MONKS A stave is loose in the sky barrel.
      Wash, rain
      Our scabbed sour lips.

HELMSMAN Third timefall. A rainbow. Wind shifts west.

MONKS Combed hues of haar.
      The sea girl
      Is bent over a glass of rain.

HELMSMAN Prime. They scrape thick salt from the ropes.

MONKS Think. We used to burn the sea with fires
      For a thimble of salt,
      Blackbirds and buttercups on the bank above.

HELMSMAN A herring shoal under the keel. Fifth hourfall. They fling a net.

MONKS We sink a bunch of holes for fish
      As stars harpoon
      The black whale, night.

HELMSMAN Terce. A piece of wrack astern, a skull, fabric. They cross hands.

MONKS What were you, loom-fruit, rag?
        What bone and spirit
        Did you grace once?

HELMSMAN Last sand grains. Sun high. A jostle of mackerel to port. They lower hooks.

MONKS Come, little fishes, enter
        The House of Man.
        Hook, knife, fire, pot, bellies.

HELMSMAN Sext. The glass is full of light – turn it. A blue sea circle. It rises, a whale!

MONKS A blue hill, it lunges, it sprouts
        A crystal tree.
        It sinks, a hundred gray circles.

HELMSMAN Sea fog. Prow a whisper, lost. Nones.

MONKS The blind giant, Fog,
        Gathers us,
        A troop of praising ghosts.

HELMSMAN Clear again. Wind freshening. A risen sea.

MONKS That was one bruiser of a wave!
        It set me on my knees.
        Wave broke and knelt: sea orisons.

HELMSMAN Vespers. Sea sifting in. Salt sift, first shadows. They bail with pans.

MONKS Foam on rowlocks, like lace
        At a bishop's sleeve,
        Swift flowers of the cherry.

HELMSMAN Fourth sandfall. Clear sky, falling wind, showers on horizon.

MONKS One bale for a princess in Tara,
        Blue silk.
        Then rags, the beggars of Clare passing through.

HELMSMAN Compline. Supper of herring. A new moon.

MONKS A young bull, silver-horned.

The moon
Grazes on dew-of-spindrift.
HELMSMAN Glass brimmed with shadows. Sunset. All's well.
MONKS All's well. Praise God. We kneel,
We cross hands.
The watchman waketh. Brother Night,
fold us.

Scene 9 THE MAN ON THE ROCK

BROTHER BRIAN *reads And they came to a great rock standing in the sea, and thereon sat a naked man in full great misery and pain, for the waves of the sea had so beaten his body that all the flesh was gone off, and left nothing but sinews and bare bones. And when the waves were gone, there was a canvas . . . which beat his body full sore with the blowing of the wind.*

Miserere of the sea, the cry of a wave on a solitary rock.

FINN There's a poor place, if ever there was one – a rock sticking out of the sea, and some seabirds.

COLM Sail right past the rock, Cormac.

CORMAC What a tumult the gulls are making now!

LIAM Surely – no, it can't be – is that a *man* on the face of the crag, high up there?

EAMON It is. A fowler after birds and eggs. He has a bag on his shoulder, and ropes round him.

BRANDON Brother Cormac.

CORMAC What is it, Brandon?

BRANDON I want to speak to that man on the crag. We'll never have the chance again. Now don't be frightened. Do you know who that man is?

CORMAC No, Brandon.

MALACHI We've all seen a fowler before.

BRANDON I suppose some of you have heard the name of Judas Iscariot.

THE MONKS Of course we have, Brandon . . . He's the man that betrayed the Lord for thirty pieces of silver . . . A black scoundrel he was . . . He went and hanged himself on a tree.

BRANDON There he is, on that cliff. Judas Iscariot. Sail in close, Cormac. Don't be frightened.

MALACHI Oh no! I don't think I can stand much more of this fantasy.

MICHAEL He's a fowler, Brandon.

BRANDON Brothers, you don't know very much, do you? You think Judas is burning in the deepest pit of hell forever. Well, he is. But Judas gets a day off occasionally – some scholars think once a year, others think every Sunday and every feast day.

He calls Hello, you up there on the rock!

MAN ON THE ROCK Hello! – I have nothing for you, sailors. The eggs are for the laird. I have to gather a full bag before night . . . Get off, gulls!

BRANDON Listen, Judas – tell us – what are you doing in this place?

MAN ON THE ROCK What?

BRANDON Why are you on the rock here?

MAN ON THE ROCK I *have* to come, one day in every year. It's a devil of a job. I'm the only one who knows how to scale the crag. So I'm the laird's egg-man. They'll soon be coming to fetch me. Thank the Lord. I'm covered in bird-lime. They always come for me at sunset in the yawl.

BRANDON What did I tell you, brothers? It's Judas. One day a year, Satan lets him out of hell. Whether that's an act of mercy or an added punishment, the scholars can't agree. In one sense, his day off must underline the horror of his perpetual prison of fire. For after a time the damned will get used a little to the scaldings of hell – won't they? It must no longer seem so terrible to them. But Judas here, lashed with spray and eaten with cold – how extra dreadful the fire must seem to him when he's thrust back into it! And believe me, brothers, for certain of the damned, such as Pilate, Herod, Caiaphas, and Judas, the hottest hobs of hell are set apart.

MAN ON THE ROCK You down there – sailors – do you see a small boat on the horizon?

BRANDON What did Judas say then, brother?

PADRAIG He's wondering if his mates are coming to take him home.

BRANDON The demons. Well then, I think we can do this poor wretched creature a good turn – though he doesn't deserve it, of course.

MARTIN He'll be glad of his turf fire and his mulled ale this cold day.

A plashing of oars. A small boat comes into view round the cliff, with two oarsmen in her.

FIRST OARSMAN Hello, sailors! Where are you bound? Not much trade on a bare island like this.

SECOND OARSMAN They're not sailors. Look at the cowls. They're monks.

FIRST OARSMAN So they are . . . Jocelyn, how many eggs have you got? Here we are, man. Climb down. We'll soon have you home.

BRANDON *to the oarsmen* Begone, fiends! Begone, creatures of darkness!

MICHAEL Brandon, you'll frighten them.

SEAMUS They look like honest folk to me – farm labourers, I think.

BRANDON Begone! I'm not afraid of you. You aren't Lucifer or Beelzebub. You're just the scivvies and scullions of hell.

FIRST OARSMAN Father Abbot – if that's what you are – we've come to fetch Jocelyn the fowler back to the hall . . . Come on down now, Jocelyn. Be careful. Reach out a hand to Jocelyn there. Careful with the eggs.

BRANDON Look at them, brothers. Fallen angels. Behold and tremble . . .

Loudly to the boatmen.

Return, accursed ones, to the pit of Gehenna. This poor soul – wicked though he was in his life, none wickeder – will have a second day out in the wind and the spray. Go on now, away back to Gehenna with you.

MAN ON THE ROCK My arms are numb. Pay no attention to that old idiot. Get me into the boat.

SECOND OARSMAN Jocelyn, I'm sorry. We daren't take you. The holy abbot will put a curse on us.

MAN ON THE ROCK *I can't stay here all night.* I'll fall off the rock. I'll get broken to pieces. The birds'll eat me.

FIRST OARSMAN Monks on a ship – who ever heard the like! Come on, Simon, row back. We'll tell the laird.

SECOND OARSMAN There's nothing we can do, Jocelyn, against fourteen holy half-mad mariners.

The oars plash, find a rhythm, diminish.

MAN ON THE ROCK Come back! For pity's sake.

BRANDON Poor Judas – see how miserable he is, even on his day of respite . . . Judas, you can bide on the ledge one night more. Don't be afraid. The devils have gone now. Enjoy the cold. Try and sleep if you can.

MAN ON THE ROCK *Hell and blast and damnation.*

LIAM Brandon, Judas – the folk in the boat called him Jocelyn the fowler – whatever his name is, he doesn't seem to be pleased about something.

BRANDON His nature, brother. Out of the mouth of such a one come only curses, even when they ought to be glad and grateful.

MAN ON THE ROCK *enraged* Why couldn't you mind your own business, you bald-heads! I could be home in the kitchen now, with a mug of hot ale and a bannock! I'd be sitting at the fire with Mara, the girl that sweeps the hearth.

BRANDON Be quiet, Judas. Listen, poor tormented soul. It's dark. The brothers are going to sing vespers now. I'm sure you never thought you'd hear such a blessed sound again. Then we'll all go to sleep.

The Man on the Rock's cry of despair is taken up and lost in the monks' night-song.

THE MONKS
Come, first star. Bring
Your hundreds and thousands.
To the innocent
The star is a honeydrop of delight.
To him who has worked evil under the sun
A needle of torment.

Dawn. The monks asleep in the ship. The Man on the Rock is gray with cold and rigid with cramps.

The small boat approaches – this time the laird is in her as well as the oarsmen.

LAIRD Jocelyn, are you there? Are you all right, man?

MAN ON THE ROCK I don't know, master. I could be dead. I'm cold and stiff enough.

LAIRD Are the eggs safe?

MAN ON THE ROCK I lost interest in eggs and birds soon after midnight, master.

FIRST OARSMAN Look – a lot of yellow splashes on the rock down below, master.

LAIRD Jocelyn, you idiot, the eggs are all broken! I've a good mind to leave you where you are.

MAN ON THE ROCK Please, master. I've had nothing to eat since yesterday but a piece of seaweed and a limpet.

LAIRD Is this the ship of monks you were telling me about?

MAN ON THE ROCK I'll work without wages till I die. Only take me off.

SECOND OARSMAN Yes, master. It's the floating abbey.

LAIRD Ho, you there in the ship! What's your game, eh? What do you mean, interfering with my fowlers and boatmen? . . . All right then, Jocelyn, jump on board. Rub his hands, you. Put the bottle between his teeth. They're clacking like ice . . .

Shouting up at the ship I'm expecting the bishop soon. He'll be told about this.

MAURICE That one sounds as wild as the devil himself, Brandon.

LAIRD Turn the boat round. No pickled gulls' eggs next winter. Jocelyn, I might have to dock some of your wages. Hurry now – get away from that ship of fools.

The oars' strokes diminish.

LAIRD *shouting back* Don't ever darken the door of my hall with your begging bowls!

BRANDON *wakening* What a terrible noise on the water, brothers! What about Judas? He's gone. They must have come for him. I wonder if we should have been so kind to Judas. They'll probably give him an extra thrashing when they get him home to hell.

MAN ON THE ROCK *his voice thin with distance.*

Madmen!

BRANDON Was that Judas shouting? *Madmen* – was that what he called us? Well, he would. To evil men, men who try to be good must seem mad.

MALACHI How much longer, this mad voyage?

Scene 10   THE MOUNTAIN OF FIRE

BROTHER BRIAN *reads And then there came a south wind and drove the ship northward, whereas they saw an island full dark and full of stench and smoke, and there they heard great blowing and blasting of bellows, but they might see nothing, but heard great thundering, whereof they were sore afeard, and blessed them oft.*

A roaring of flame, hiss of steam, crashing of ice about the sea quest.

FINN   Brother, look. In the north-west there – low down – fire!

MAURICE   A burning mountain!

CORMAC   South wind for six days. We've never been as far north as this.

LIAM   Pillars of crystal big as churches. The darkness.

EAMON   The saints keep us from that burning shore ahead!

PADRAIG   The ship's driving straight at it.

CORMAC   The rudder's useless. We must go where the wind takes us.

MARTIN   If only we could see the sun! There's only this little gray between the two darknesses.

MICHAEL   Brandon, father, where are we?

BRANDON   Little brothers, be strong and quiet. Have courage a little longer. You've been good sailors, good pilgrims, for six years now.

MALACHI   Seven months. The liar. But it's long enough.

BRANDON   You must be very brave now. Don't ask me. To say the name of the shore we're coming to would put black terror on you all.

SEAMUS   Turn the ship back! We'll be burned and drowned – crushed in the crystal pillars!

CORMAC   I'm *trying* to turn her. The helm won't answer.

BRANDON   Be brave. Be thankful. We're certain, after this, to set foot on the Isle of the Blessed. This is a pledge and a promise.

Brandon shouts at the fire on the horizon Burn on, Blackness! Flame! Gates of Hell!

SEAN But what's the name of the place, Brandon?

CORMAC Iceland is somewhere hereabout. Look at the chart. 'Here be volcanoes, snow, hills of fire'.

COLM I've heard there's Irish monks in Iceland.

BRANDON Sail in as close as you can. Behold the shores of Hell. Inside that mountain the damned feast on each other. They gnaw eyeballs. They sit in dark flames. They claw each other, naked and foul. Yet each one is locked in his own torture and shame forever. Multitudes, reeking multitudes. Each soul locked in lonely everlasting pain. Imagine a honeycomb, brothers, seething with acid, sulphur, slime, pus, wormwood, rot, mildew, rust, phlegm, scab, weevil, dung, mould, measel-rose, deathsweat. That's what Hell is . . . There they stand, look at them, with their burning throats, the high lords of Hell, guarding that immense dungeon – Mephistopheles, Lucifer, Asmodeus, Belial and the rest.

Burn on, Satan! Yell and belch there. I'm not frightened of you! We are holding up our crosses.

They can't singe a hair of your head, brothers. Hold your crosses up high.

The monks, all the same, begin to wail and whimper and pray.

Sail in closer, Cormac. See, they're dropping their fireballs all round the ship now. Never mind. Sail on. We'll squander them, the hell hounds.

Increasing thunder and flame from the island ahead.

Suddenly Brother Malachi has some kind of fit. He begins to rail and foam and scream at Brandon.

MALACHI You old fool! How much longer do I have to put up with you! You'll be the death of everyone in this ship!

FINN Malachi, you mustn't speak like that to our abbot.

MALACHI *dropping his voice* Listen, my friends. Where are we supposed to be headed? The Island of the Blessed. You'll never get there. There is no Island of the Blessed. If there was, why haven't we reached it before now? We're blundering round and round this sea in circles. We haven't been further than a few islands round Ireland and Scotland – the Blaskets, Tory, Rockall, Hirta, Barra, Hoy – places like that. Blown back and fore on every wind, with a madman in command. The Island of the Dog – that was a laugh! – a cur barking round a deserted croft . . . What was the next piece of lunacy – Jascoyne – he forced us to light a fire on a whale's back . . . And then – O Lord! – rooks in a tree singing Matins and Vespers, if you please. Nobody heard the psalms but himself. He's crazy, I tell you. He's getting worse . . . A poor fowler taking eggs from a cliff – who was he but Judas Iscariot! – of course he *had* to be, according to Brandon . . . And now Hell. It's Iceland, brothers, the island with the volcanoes. It's on the chart here, plainly marked: Iceland, *Iceland*, ICELAND . . . We'll all be as crazy as Brandon if this voyage goes on. I wish he would die. I wish the sea would take the old fool. A whole year wasted, when I could have been working on my manuscripts back home in Ireland, in my little cell, with a candle burning. A whole twelvemonth made barren, because of the delusions of a madman . . .

He shrieks Madness and death! – that'll be the end of us. Madness, destruction.

MAURICE Seize Malachi! He's foaming at the mouth. Hold him down.

MALACHI *whimpering* Father Brandon, have great pity on me. Forgive the terrible things I've said. I've never seen on this earth such goodness as yours. It's that goodness that fills me with rage and hatred. Dear Brandon, I'm sorry. Pray for me.

BRANDON Malachi, child, I warned you well not to come on this voyage. You were too clever. Pray for innocence.

MALACHI I can't pray. I haven't been able to pray on this sea – not once.

He begins to yell again I've fallen into the power of the dog!

He breaks free I hate you all! I hate this ship! I hate the voyage! I hate everything, everybody! I hate my life! Let me go.

With a cry Brother Malachi leaps into the sea.

The monks cross themselves. They murmur fragments: 'De profundis clamavi, Domine . . .'

CORMAC He's lost, Brandon. He's clutching at ice. He's drinking the sea. There, he's sunk! A hand. It vanished.

BRANDON *in an altered voice* An old crazy man.

LIAM A bubble on the surface. Malachi's gone under. He's drowned.

THE MONKS Requiescat. Requiescat. Requiescat.

CORMAC The wind's gone right round, Brandon. It's in the north now. We're sailing away from Hell.

BRANDON Is it? The wind in the north. Well, I suppose we'd better go where the wind takes us. Iceland. Did somebody say Iceland? Brothers, fancy that – we've sailed as far as Iceland. Did somebody say a man was lost? Drowned? The Icelanders are good folk. They'll bury his body on the shore.

THE MONKS Yes, Brandon.

BRANDON Drowned, is he? Intelligence is gone from this ship. It's a ship of fools now. I'm beginning to be tired of winds and waters. I feel very old, brothers. The burning throats of Hell . . . What were we speaking about, the wind? The wind. The wind was in the south and now it's in the north. Iceland, Ireland. Some day soon there'll be a west wind, and then we'll sail home to Ireland, brothers. It won't be before time.

Brothers, I confess to you now that I've led you on a fool's voyage. Round and round, in salt and seaweed, a circle of madness. Set sail for Ireland and the abbey. What will we find there? For you it will be home and peace and sanity. I look – God help me – for death. The drained honeycomb. I'm an old foolish man. Sail on, whithersoever.

Scene 11 THE OLD MAN WHO LIVES BESIDE A BURN

BROTHER BRIAN *reads And after, St Brandon sailed southwards three days and three nights, and on the Friday they saw an island, and then St Brandon began to sigh, and said: I see the island wherein St Paul the hermit dwelleth, and hath dwelled these forty years without meat and drink ordained by man's hand.*

The ship is anchored beside a bare island.

Brother Liam comes out of a cave with a little sack containing hearts of kale.

Brandon has a gray face and a gray voice.

BRANDON I don't want to hear whom you've seen or what you've met. Put the sack in the well. Go to your place, Liam.

LIAM Yes, Father Brandon. It's cabbages.

BRANDON My sole concern is to get us back to Ireland. Understand that. No more angels or demons or marvels. The voyage home, nothing more.

CORMAC Yes, Father.

BRANDON There's an old man in this island, I know. I saw him. I know the kind of man that would be set down on a barren rock like this. Thieves and murderers. Mutineers. Lepers. More likely he was just a sailor. His ship struck in a storm, only he got ashore. A long time ago. A common enough thing.

FERGUS Yes, Father.

BRANDON What have you got in the sack, Liam?

LIAM A few cabbages, Brandon. A few hearts of kale. The old man has a hut and a yard.

BRANDON I don't want to know about him. He sold you kale. Coins for cabbages. Fair enough. No more.

LIAM There's nothing to tell, Father. The old man's dumb as a stone.

BRANDON Is he? Good. We'll soon all be dumb as stones. Good.

There's too much talk in the world – wild whirling foolish words.
Dumb as skulls, soon, Good. Good.
 Hoist the sail.

LIAM There's a little burn goes past the old man's door, Father,
with an otter and a trout in it.

BRANDON No more. I told you. Enough. 'Paul the hermit!' You all
expected me to cry 'Paul the hermit!' as soon as we sighted this rock.

Brandon's voice moves into a mock-pious chant.

Paul the hermit abode in the monastery of St Patrick.
He was a famous confessor.
Folk travelled on all the roads of Ireland for to be shriven of Paul
the confessor. He knew their sins before their mouths were
 unlocked.
Cometh the Abbot of St Patrick to Paul the confessor.
'Paul, there's a boat waiting for thee, down at the rock.
Sail west, Paul, sail west.'
Paul findeth the boat, west he urgeth oar, he cometh to an isle of the
 ocean, sans water and food.
Cometh out of ocean to Paul an otter, that beareth in its foreclaws a
 flintstone and a bit of iron.
What gleam in the otter's mouth, what shineth there? A fish.
The otter setteth all at the feet of the saint.
Then Paul kindleth flame, and broileth the fish,
And the fish was a clean bone three days after.
Then cometh the otter again, with kindling and a fat sweet fish,
A three-day feast.
And this three-day courtesy of beast and fish and fire and man hath
 gone on, a sweet monotony, for a hundred years.

LIAM Is that so, Father?

BRANDON No. It is *not*. Paul the hermit never existed. If he did,
he's rotten. It was a long time ago. Words, breath, a story – an old
winter fire-side foolishness.

FERGUS The old man's on the shore now. Look! The otter's
trotting after him like a dog. Is that a harp in the old man's hand?

COLM It's a bunch of fish. He's offering them to us.

BRANDON My good man, I know you can't speak our language –
but listen.

Music between the shore and the ship.

LIAM The old man isn't dumb at all. He's saying, 'Take the fish,
sailors.'
BRANDON *gritting his teeth* The old man said nothing *He said nothing.*
LIAM Yes, he did, Father. I heard him. Sweet as a lark he sang.
BRANDON How is it that you, Liam – a tinker boy – can hear things
your Abbot Brandon can't hear? It's I, Brandon, that used to hear
words where none were. Never again.
    Did the old man speak, brothers, or did he not?
MAURICE There was a kind of a sound, Father.
MARTIN Like a harp stroke it was, Father.
CORMAC But no words. No words.
FERGUS Not a word in the world that I heard. Liam heard words.
BRANDON Take the fish, Seamus. The old man's arm must be
tired with holding out the few fish ... We thank you, old
shipwrecked sailor, for the fish.

Thin music, again.

BRANDON Old man, come closer. My monks here, they thought a
while back you might be Paul the famous hermit. Are you Paul the
hermit? Don't bother speaking. Just shake your head. Then,
chastened, we'll turn the ship round. We'll leave you in peace.

The sea between island and boat brims with sound. The monks listen, leaning forward,
putting hands to ears. Only Brandon hears nothing but the wash of sea through stones.

BRANDON
No use. He's witless as well as dumb.
What are you all gaping at?
Goodbye, my good man.
Up anchor, Cormac.
MONKS *together* No, Father ... Listen ... Oh please be quiet, you're
spoiling everything ... Listen ... Such loveliness ...
BRANDON I'm master on this ship. Go to your places every man.

MONKS Shut him up! . . . Stop his jaw, the old fool . . . Listen, listen.

Music still: it resumes, sweetens, dwindles into lucent echoes.

MONKS Please . . . Please, more . . . Strike the harp of your mouth again . . . No, my flesh would melt if I heard more. A little, maybe.

BRANDON *sternly* Brothers!

FERGUS What an ugly sound, like a frog. Ugh! Shut up.

SEAN It's Brandon. His mouth's opening and shutting.

BRANDON That old man said not a word. He's standing on the shore with a vacant look on his face. He's half-witted, I tell you.

FINN Didn't you hear him? You must have heard him, Father . . . Didn't you hear the fine poetry that came from him, like honey from the side of a lion?

COLM The like I never heard.

MICHAEL It was like an angel speaking.

LIAM Yes, and the otter spoke too. I'm sure of it. And the fish.

FERGUS No, I didn't hear the fish.

LIAM The stones sang too. Listen. It's still going on.

BRANDON Cormac, I told you some time ago to weigh anchor.

CORMAC What did the man sing, Liam? Tell us. We heard the music but not the words.

BRANDON Liam, you are not to speak. I am your abbot. I command you. Clean the fish over the side, Liam. You're a tinker boy, good with a knife. Gut the fish.

The monks cluster about Liam.

LIAM He said . . .

BRANDON *Go back to your places. I command you. I am your abbot. No more of this nonsense.*

Brandon takes two monks by the shoulders.

MARTIN Take you hands from me! I'm trying to listen to Liam.

MAURICE Stick a gag in Brandon's old mouth!

Brandon is beaten. He turns his back on the ship's company. He puts his hands to his face.

SEAN What did the man say, Liam?

LIAM He said, 'Yes, I'm Paul the hermit. Also I'm Molloy the shipwrecked sailor. And I'm Fingal the thief, too, put ashore for my crimes. I'm a fisherman too old to catch fish, but this otter helps me. I'm a pirate, too; I'm guarding a hoard of gold. I'm a prince exiled by his wicked brother. I'm a tinker tired of travelling. I'm Byrne the poet and I'm Bran the beachcomber and I'm Flynn the fowler. I'm a boy. I'm the woman that bakes and combs her hair and waits beside the rock. I'm Everyman.

My circle of time is rounding back upon itself. I'm old. I reach out my withered hand to touch the fingers of a child. Within the bright circle that is a man multitudes move, like the crowd in Sligo on a market day, only more, many many more. Inside the circle I am saint and sinner. Yes, and I am every gentle innocent creature, I am otter and fish and stone and shell and seawead, I am cloud and rockpool, I am fire . . . I contain within myself an entire universe. This it is to be a man.

Yet, at the time of death, just as the circle closes, one out of that multitude goes free. He sets out on the long purgatorial journey back to God, the journey that began before birth.

Tell that to your abbot Brandon: if Brandon still has ears to hear.'

CORMAC That was the very music of his speech.

LIAM It sounds very dull on my tongue. 'Tell that to Brandon,' says he. 'Cheer him up. Brandon doesn't look happy today. Tell Brandon,' says he 'I'm glad he came. Now go, all of you, go with God.'

BRANDON I heard nothing – only the waves on the rock. Little Brothers, why could I hear nothing?

MARTIN Isn't it a wonder Brandon could hear nothing?

FERGUS A bitter shame indeed.

SEAN A strength went out of Brandon after Iceland. He isn't himself.

MAURICE Yes, after Malachi was lost in the ice.

BRANDON *calling* Paul! Paul the hermit!

COLM He's turned his back, Father. He doesn't hear you.

BRANDON Just say one word, Paul. A blessing.

The man on the island turns. He holds up his hand. Music.

BRANDON *humble* Yes, I understand. Oh, thank you. We'll go there if you say so. Thank you for these words, Father Paul, I'll treasure them always. Thank you for the fish too. Thank you for opening the scar on my spirit, though it hurts, it hurts like wounds and death.

CORMAC But the old man never said a word to Brandon.

FERGUS I heard nothing either.

SEAMUS Why is Brandon weeping? Look at the diamonds and the pearls on his face.

COLM A treasure, surely.

BRANDON Brothers, I was nearly lost and sunk between Iceland and here. The good gift of imagination, it was taken from me. I thank you, brothers, and that old man, for saving me in time. You're right, such music I never heard. It ravished my soul.

LIAM What did he say to you, Brandon?

BRANDON What did he say? How will I find the words? That a blessing is no selfish dew. It brightens no solitary head and heart. It falls through time, continuously. It shimmers like dew on the whole web of creation. Always, everywhere. If it weren't so, the whole world would long ago be ice and ashes.

Then he blessed us and our ship and our voyage. That is, he blessed the whole world and its travail.

FERGUS It was worth coming all this way, to hear just that one old man alone.

COLM It was; thanks be to God.

CORMAC Now we can turn the ship towards Ireland.

BRANDON Not yet, Cormac. He said, 'The Island of the Young is just under the horizon, a day's sail westward.' We must sail there, to round out our voyage. 'Only', (said Paul) 'don't expect a place where time is one single unsullied crystal. The dew fell on Eden sweeter after the flaws and the fractures wrecked the garden.'

EAMON Well now, look at *that*!

LIAM What is it, Eamon?

EAMON The otter. It's lighting a fire of sticks down there. Look at the flame in its paw!

HERMIT *I Paul bless you and your voyage, Everyman. Go forward.*

Scene 12   TIR-NAN-OG

BROTHER BRIAN *reads And . . . it began to hail right fast, and therewith came a dark mist which lasted long after, which feared St Brandon and his monks, and they prayed to our Lord to keep and help them . . . And soon after that mist passed away, and anon they saw the fairest country (westward) that any man might see, and it was so clear and bright that it was a heavenly sight to behold, and all the trees were charged with ripe fruit, and herb full of flowers . . . And there came to them a fair young man and welcomed them courteously.*

Brandon and the monks have come to the shore of Tir-Nan-Og, The Isle of the Ever-Young.

The brothers sing.

We thank you, Lord.
After the seven-year sackcloth quest,
Here we stand
At last on the shore of Tir-Nan-Og.
The beach-stones (diamonds)
Feel sharp and cold to our sinful feet.
Patch has slipped on a strand of seaweed (pure silk)
And wet his bum.

Our eyes survey
The endless summer skies of Tir-Nan-Og
But our sinful cheeks
Shrink from the usual rain and wind,
A filthy rag of cloud in the west.
At last we have stumbled
On the Isle of the Ever-Young.

A stone comes crashing down from a cliff top among the monks; then another.

EAMON   What was that?
CORMAC   Take shelter. Pieces of the cliff are falling down.

Three more stones crash down. The monks scatter, all but Brandon who stays where he is.

BRANDON Blessed be this island.

ISLANDER You down there – Pirates! Get away from here. Go on now – back to your ship.

Another stone.

There's nothing for you here – just stones. We'll give you all the stones you want.

BRANDON Blessed be the stones.

MAURICE Brandon, don't stand there. Come in here, into the cave. That stone just missed you.

ISLANDER Just you try, pirates, to come up this cliff. You see the path up the cliff? You can only come up one at a time. We're here waiting for you, a score of us. Down you'll go a lot quicker than you came up.

CORMAC Brandon, let's go back to the ship.

MARTIN No, we must get bread and water somehow. The hold's empty. We've nothing to eat or drink.

CORMAC If only that idiot up there didn't keep shouting about pirates. *He calls* Hey, you up there. We're monks from Ireland, not pirates. We need provisions. We've got money. We want to do business with you.

Another stone is flung down. It breaks in pieces beside Brandon.

ISLANDER Make bread out of that, pirates.

BRANDON Blessed be the stone and the dust.

SEAN *We're Irish monks.*

ISLANDER What's that? Monks? Oh, are you? The last ship that came here, she was supposed to be a Spanish merchant ship. A cargo of leather and oranges, bound for Norway. We had a terrible time with that bunch of cut-throats. They robbed our harvest.

BRANDON Blessed be the fruits of the island.

ISLANDER They did worse than that to the women. What's that old villain singing about, down there?

137

Another falling bounding shattering stone.

I'll put a stop to his singing, the thief. There's plenty of stones up here. I'll crush his skull.

MAURICE He's putting a blessing on your island, man. He's a very holy monk. He's our abbot, Brandon.

ISLANDER Is he? He doesn't seem to be scared, right enough. Them pirates turned out to be terrible cowards, once we turned the tables on them . . . Monks, eh? And you're wanting some food. You'll have to pay for it. No charity here, we can't afford it, it's been a poor harvest.

COLM Martin, show him a gold piece. Make it flash in the sun.

FERGUS Gold melts the heart quicker than blessings.

ISLANDER All right. Gold. We *might* do business with you. I'll see what my men say. We're promising nothing. We could have some apples and corn to spare in the loft.

BRANDON Blessed be the boughs and the barn.

ISLANDER Listen, you down there. We still don't trust you. So don't all come crowding up the cliff at once. The old man that's singing – tell him to come up, alone.

LIAM Don't go, Brandon. They'll kill you. They'll throw you off the cliff-top. They're savages.

ISLANDER And let him take the money in his hand. No gold, no grub. Tell him to hurry. We've got work to do.

Brandon begins to climb up the crag face.

MONKS Be careful, Brandon . . . It's very steep . . . Watch where you put your foot, now . . .

MAURICE We never got a reception like this before, any place we've been to.

COLM Tir-Nan-Og indeed! A poor bleak place. Did you ever see such stony fields?

SEAN The houses – they're hardly better than styes.

MARTIN Brandon, don't look down!

CORMAC Paul the hermit was wrong. He said the next island we came to would be the Earthly Paradise.

SEAMUS How did the old writers describe the place in their parchments?

BRIAN 'In that island is joy and mirth enough, and the earth of that island shineth as bright as the sun, and there are the fairest trees and herbs that ever any man saw, and there were many precious stones shining bright, and every herb there was full of flowers, and every tree full of fruit, so that it was a glorious sight and a heavenly joy to abide there. And there, there came to them a fair young man, and full courteously he welcomed them all . . .'

The monks laugh.

CORMAC But Brandon too, he said this was the place. As soon as he saw it black against the sunset last night. He began to sing. He sang praises of the island all night long.

FERGUS He's never done singing since. He's like a tree in April.

MARTIN There now. Brandon's reached the top. Thank goodness. The man's giving him a hand.

The cliff top.

ISLANDER Give us your hand, old man. Here you are. Sit down on the grass till you get your breath.

BRANDON Deo gratias.

ISLANDER I can see you're a monk all right, not a pirate. We have to be careful, Father. You understand that. We've had so much trouble from ships.

BRANDON Blessed be the cargoes that come to the island.

ISLANDER It isn't as if the place was fertile, it isn't. Cold grudging clay. It's a marvel that corn roots in it at all.

BRANDON Blessed be the seed-time.

ISLANDER Last harvest was the worst I ever remember. A few wet gray sheaves. It rained for a solid month, Father.

To the island women Here, you women, what are you gaping at? You've seen a monk before. That ship down there, it needs provisioning. So get a barrel of apples out of the loft, and a few sacks of meal. The monks are needing cheese and cider too. Round up a few of the geese you're keeping for Christmas. Hurry up, now.

The women go away chattering.

It isn't a rich island you've come to, Father. Clay and rock. One day of rain and every field's a quagmire.

He calls.

Andrew, Martin, Philip – put away them flails. Or rather, take them to the barn and thresh a sheaf or two. You're not needed here. They're not pirates. They're holy mariners.

The farm workers go off.

My tenants, Father. They're the laziest craftiest folk in the world. You wouldn't believe the things they get up to. I try to treat them all decently. That stretch of good land on the hill over there – I shared it out as fairly as I could – every man has his own rig. And I don't interfere with their women, like some of the lairds used to do in the old days – you know, the right of the bridal bed. Nothing like that. And they can take as much fish out of the sea as they like, and seaweed too. (I only take one fish in every seven.) I try to be fair to them, Father. Whenever there's any danger, I'm their shield and their sword. Like today, you saw how the island was suddenly a fortress, till we realized that you weren't pirates at all, but monks. (What are you doing so far west anyway, Father? Well, never mind just now.) And whenever they come to blows, about a girl maybe or a gannet, it's me that has to be judge and peace-maker. You'd think they'd show some kind of gratitude for all I do for them. Not a bit. When it comes to rent-time, the barrels are empty! the cupboards are bare! Nothing but whines and complaints. 'A poor year at the fishing,' they say, 'your honour . . . The fulmars were never scarcer on the cliff, sorry . . .' I can hardly get them off their backsides to come and cut my barley – that's part of their duty too, Father. I only got them to the cliff today because I mentioned 'a ship'. At once they thought of wrecks – barrels of wine, planks of wood. That's the kind of folk they are. This is the community I have the care and keeping of.

And the women, Father. You never saw such lazy bitches. In my father's time they did their work in a way – spinning and making cloth, you know, and baking and brewing and scouring their floors. These young women don't want to do a thing. All they think about is, when will the next ship drop anchor out there? You saw how disgusted they were when they knew you were monks. Well, that's the way it is. That's my house over there, Father. The Hall. Well, of course it's a lot bigger and better than the cottages. And the fields too – it's only right that the laird has the best land in the place. He has a lot of expenses, with one thing and another. Dignity doesn't come cheap. All the horses in that field belong to me, and the bull. The mill up there, it's mine of course.

We're a very old family. I don't know how long it is since we came to this island. The first ancestor I know anything about, he was called, oddly enough, MacAdam. Since then we've had our ups and downs. We try to keep a vestige of pride, in spite of everything. Our heraldry is cut over the door – an apple and an adder and a burning sword – and one word, *Endure*.

I want you, Father, to have a look at the church over there. Oh, never fear, he won't trouble you, the priest. He's not too keen to meet holy men. That man, Father, he's the biggest thorn of all in my flesh. He is. He does nothing all winter but drink ale and play his fiddle. In summer he's down at the rock, fishing. Fish, fish, from morning to night. His church couldn't have a better name, St Peter's. Well, that man, as soon as the miller has tied up the last sack of meal, along he comes and claims *one-tenth*, as of right. The kirk's share, the tithe, says he. And he's never so much as flashed a scythe among the ripe corn, not once. I must admit, though, Father, that he's a good fiddler. The winters here would be gloomier without him. He makes the old men dance like boys. The islanders seem to like him. I suppose he eases their pangs and their rages, in a sort of a way, here in Hirta. He puts peace on their comings and kissings and goings.

BRANDON Blessed be the Isle of the Ever-Young.

ISLANDER Here they come now with your provisions, Father. What's that you've got there, Maria – mussels, is it? I hope you

picked the best ones out of the pool for Father Brandon here.
That's a good girl. And cider, good. Be careful with the barrel, lads.
The monks, they'll relish a drop of apple wine on the way home.
There's worse things than cider. (Did I tell you how we captured the
pirates, Father? – we made them drunk on cider one night.) And
meal – seven bags – that's the stuff, well done. Carry it down the
crag. Martin, you go first, show them the way. I don't want them
tearing the sacks on the stones.

BRANDON Blessed be the stone, the wind, the dew.

ISLANDER You can have a few big stones too, Father, if you think
they're so precious. Ballast.

No, Father, I wouldn't dream of it. Just you put that money back
in your purse. I don't know when I've enjoyed a visit so much. I like
some intelligent conversation now and again.

You've put enough blessings on our island to last to the end of
time. We'll be needing them all, I wouldn't wonder.

Bless you too, Father. Watch where you put your foot now. I think
it would be better if I was to go down the crag first. You follow me.
Easy now. A hand there. That's the way. It's a pleasure.

Brandon and the monks on the shore. The cargo being taken from island to ship.

BRANDON I suppose you know what island this is, brothers.

CORMAC We know and we don't know.

MAURICE Whatever it was before, Brandon, you've put so many
blessings on it, from now on it's bound to be called The Island of the
Blessed.

COLM It's a poor-like place, all the same.

BRANDON Thank God our eyes have seen it at last. This is what
we've come all this way for: to see man, in his little kingdom, in all
his frailty and glory.

CORMAC Brandon, the stores are on board now.

COLM The wind's due west, Brandon. It's blowing towards Ireland.

BRANDON Well, then, hoist the sail.

CORMAC Up anchor! Hoist the sail!

BRANDON Brother Brian, the scribe, I have something to say to
you.

BRIAN I'm listening, Father.

BRANDON Once we get back to Ireland, your task will be to write down the story of this voyage.

BRIAN I know. I'll do my best. I've been making a note now and again.

BRANDON We'll speak about it sometime. No voyage is ever what it seems to be.

Surge of sea from the prow.

CORMAC I can smell shamrocks in the wind!

MONKS We're going home!

BRANDON Blessed be the voyage.

Scene 13 THE DEATH OF BRANDON

BROTHER BRIAN *reads And then they took their ship and came home to Ireland in safety, whom their brothers received with great joy, giving thankings to our Lord which had kept them all those seven years from many a peril and brought them home in safety, to whom be given honour and glory, world without end. Amen. And soon after, this holy man St Brandon waxed feeble and sick, and had but little joy of this world, but ever after his joy and mind was in the joys of heaven.*

BRANDON Who's there? It's dark. Light the candle.

BRIAN It's me, Brandon. Brother Brian the scribe. You sent for me.

BRANDON Did I? Now what could I be wanting with Brian the scribe? I'm not feeling well today.

BRIAN Perhaps something to do with the voyage. You remember, you asked me to write an account of it.

BRANDON So I did, Brian. So I did. How cold it is on the ship today. What island are we making for now, Brian?

BRIAN Father, we're in Ireland. We came home a month ago. You're in your own abbey.

BRANDON I keep forgetting. I'm very old, Brian. Very tired. I'm not long for this world.

BRIAN Don't say that, Brandon.

BRANDON Why not? I look forward to the day of my death. On that day I'll step ashore on an island even further west than Tir-Nan-Og. Oh, to be out of this prison of bone and dust.

BRIAN What will we do without you, Father?

BRANDON Tell me now, Brian – whatever became of the ship?

BRIAN She's hauled up on the shore.

BRANDON But we got home safely. Isn't that a marvel? I can't see a thing. What's that shadow over there at the window?

BRIAN It's me, Brian.

BRANDON Byrne, is it? Not Byrne! Well, old friend, what ballad have you got for me today? I'm very pleased to see you, Byrne. How many miles have you walked since sunrise, eh? Just a verse or two.

Have you got your harp? Your poetry does my heart good, Byrne. They'll give you a bite of supper and a bed. Then at sunrise you can make a long shadow on the road.

BRIAN There, Brandon, I've lit the candle. You can see now that it's me, Brother Brian the scribe.

BRANDON Of course. I know you, Brian. What we must discuss together, you and I, Brian, is this account of our voyage. Now I remember.

BRIAN We've discussed it once or twice, Brandon, since we got back.

BRANDON Have you made a beginning yet, Brian?

BRIAN I thought I might wait till next winter, Father. Till I get things clearer in my mind.

BRANDON There's no hurry. Of course I'll be dead by then. I won't be able to read it. I want to make quite sure, while I'm still on this earth, that in your account of the voyage you make proper use of *the word*.

BRIAN The word, Brandon?

BRANDON The word. It's very important that the word should be uttered as *purely* as possible.

BRIAN I see, Brandon. I'll try.

A silence.

BRANDON What did you say? Who's there? No, it can't be! Abbot Birnius, come all this long way to see me. Have they looked after you properly, Father? Have they washed your feet? You're too old to walk all that distance over the Donegal hills. Well done. I couldn't do it myself, now. My bones are brittle and yet they're heavy as lead. What you said, Father Birnius, about The Word, is deep and subtle. I don't quite understand it. Yet it fills me with wonderment.

BRIAN I'm Brother Brian the scribe.

BRANDON Sit down, Birnius. I'm delighted to see you. The Word. Yes, what an honour has been bestowed on us both. What a responsibility too. We have been appointed, you in your abbey, Birnius, and I in mine, to be guardians of The Word.

BRIAN What word, Brandon?

BRANDON 'In principio erat verbum.' That Word. The Word that summoned creation out of chaos. Without that Word we have no understanding of anything. The Word brooded on the original tumult of darkness, that tempest of atoms, and order and pattern and meaning emerged. Of course, Birnius, what you say is very true: our finite minds, even after centuries of speculation in cloisters, can only take in a little of the meaning of The Word – one syllable perhaps – perhaps only a single letter – the rest is mystery and music. But mystery is an altogether sweeter and more blessed state than chaos, is it not? Though we can't *understand* the mystery, yet we acknowledge a divine order and pattern beyond the range of the five human senses. I think that was your argument, Birnius, the last time I saw you.

BRIAN Your cheeks are very red, Brandon. I think you must have a little fever.

BRANDON I've certainly spoken a lot. I don't think I've spoken so many words since I got home. Do you know who was here today, Birnius? You'll never guess. That old scoundrel Byrne who travels the roads with his harp. I knew him long ago, we were boys together in Mayo. Even then he could steal the heart out of your breast with his songs. And yet they were all lies . . . Where was I? What was I speaking about, Birnius? That's the way it is with old men – they babble away worse than henwives, and then they forget right away what they've said.

BRIAN You were speaking about The Divine Word, Brandon.

BRANDON Yes. Of course. The Word. *In principio erat verbum.* That Word was not uttered once for all, in the beginning. Almost from the start, Birnius – is this not so? – The Word has had its detractors – dark angels and spirits and men who sought to twist it, pervert it, turn it into The Lie. That is the business of evil, to turn The Word into The Lie . . . These abstractions – even such a marvellous abstraction as The Word – are difficult for men to grasp. We prefer the things our senses can sift and approve. And God saw with pain the perversion with which evil seeks to pervert The Word. Therefore in time he sent down The Word on earth. It lay there and cried on the straw of Bethlehem.

BRIAN It did, Brandon.

BRANDON The kingdom of evil was aware at once, of course, of the Incarnation of The Word. Herod and his horsemen rode here and there through Bethlehem with the blood of children on their swords.

BRIAN It was a pitiful thing, Brandon.

BRANDON The Incarnate Word remained hidden for a few years. Then, for a short time, it made its sweet utterances, in parable and sermon and symbol, along the shores and hills of Galilee. But finally the horsemen of the kingdom of evil came upon The Word and they seized him and they nailed him to a tree. That day the world seemed drained of all meaning. Chaos had come again. The universe was a meaningless drift of stars and atoms.

BRIAN It seemed so, Brandon.

BRANDON It only *seemed* so. How can you destroy the Creator and the creation with a few nails? One of the attributes of evil – fortunately for us, Birnius – is folly. Evil is subtle and dark and powerful and *stupid*. Three days passed. The Incarnate Word, with his five wounds on him, returned out of the heart of a stone. Easter is a time of great beauty and delight, Abbot Birnius.

BRIAN It is indeed, Brandon.

BRANDON Well then, for fifty years you and I, in our two abbeys, have been guardians of The Word. What a joy for us – what a responsibility! The Word is not an abstraction, as it was before Bethlehem, a few laws carved on stone – It is something we can touch and see and taste – It is the homeliest simplest thing imaginable, a circle of bread. So God honours in a marvellous way the labours of men in the fields, ploughman and reaper and grinder. We have had the keys of the tabernacle in our keeping for a long time, Abbot Birnius. We have tried to be faithful to our stewardship. We should be very happy.

BRIAN Brandon, I think you should get some rest. Your face is bright as a turnip lantern.

BRANDON Who's that?

BRIAN Whom do you think, Father? It's me, Brian the scribe. You sent for me. I've been here with you an hour, nobody else.

Sometimes you call me Byrne the poet. Sometimes it's Birnius, some abbot or other from Donegal. But I'm only Brian, and I'm here because you sent for me.

BRANDON Of course I want to see you, boy. About the story of our voyage. It's important it should be set down.

BRIAN It will be. I'll do my best, Brandon.

BRANDON I know you will. Have you got a sheepskin or two ready? You'll need plenty of quills, Brian, and a deep jar of ink.

BRIAN I'm all prepared, Brandon.

BRANDON Good. Well, I'm not going to tell you what to write. I leave that to the writer. (Fancy me thinking you were Byrne or Birnius! – I must have been dreaming.) All I wanted to say to you, dear Brian, is that you should exercise the utmost care in your trade. The word – written and spoken – is a good gift to us. But it is beset always, Brian, with all kinds of danger.

BRIAN That's true, Brandon.

BRANDON You should not write the story of the voyage, Brian, in strict factual terms. Such as: 'We came to an island and got a poor reception from an old ill-natured bad-tempered man who said, 'Go away, get out, I have plenty to do without feeding more mouths, I have twenty-four monks already I look after, useless creatures who can't turn a sod or light a candle, they're too lazy even to speak, and I have to dance attendance on them morning noon and night, I'm getting too old for that game, no more of that – clear off the last one of you.'

BRIAN I remember that old man and the island well, Brandon, and the abbey of twenty-four silent monks. That's what the old man said indeed. He shook his fist at us, to begin with.

BRANDON But to write that down would be to give a totally false picture of the old man and the depths of his charity. I hope, when I wear out, I'll have as shining a spirit as that old man.

BRIAN I see what you mean, Brandon.

BRANDON It won't be long. I don't feel well tonight, Brian. I'm cold, but my face is burning . . . Then there was the island where there seemed to be so many rooks in the trees. Nobody seems to like rooks or rook music. And yet God made them, and they must be good in his sight. Always, when you come to write the story, keep a little room for the creator and the creation and the harmony between them. That gift is called imagination.

BRIAN I'll try, Brandon.

BRANDON I think that's all I have to say to you now. There are people in the castles and counting-houses – very clever men, too – who have a different view of the word from you writers. When they read your manuscript, they'll sneer. They'll say, *The Voyage of Brandon* indeed – a few seedless men in a salt waste, drifting from folly to folly – no cargo or bill of lading or profit . . .

BRIAN Surely not, Brandon.

BRANDON Oh yes, they will. Never mind them. Imagine, say, a couple of country children on a roadside on a spring day. Tell the story of the voyage as if it was for their ears only. Tell it so that the children will clap their hands, and laugh, and go dancing away on the wind.

BRIAN That's a very difficult thing to do.

BRANDON There should be dew – and greenness – in every line . . . 'In the end Brandon drifted out of a last dotage and mad adventure into death' – that's what the wise wintry workaday mouths are going to say about me quite soon.

BRIAN It's them who are the fools, Brandon.

BRANDON My death, Brian – I have pains in me tonight that I never experienced before – my death will be the end of the story. When you write about my death, Brian, let there be a seed in the darkness.

Blessed be the word, Brian.

Blessed be The Word.

Amen.

Scene 14   EPILOGUE

The scribe BRIAN *reads And in a short time after St Brandon being full of virtues, departed out of his life to everlasting life, and was worshipfully buried in a fair abbey which he himself founded, where our Lord showed for this holy saint many fair miracles.*